Unmasking Kashmir

A Bureaucrat Reveals

Attention Authors

'We Convert Fighters into Writers'. That has been the motto of Manas Publications, since more than four decades. Our message to the world is that India can win the battle, not only by the bullet but also by the pen. There is no dearth of intellectuals in our country, but their knowledge is confined to them only. No sincere effort has been made by any other publisher to channelise their knowledge in national interest. That is why the talent of a large number of intellectuals, remains latent. An author transforms his knowledge, into a manuscript, and it is our job to spread his/her knowledge by converting it into a beautiful book.

For over four decades, Manas has been motivating the intellectuals by publishing their manuscripts and would like to publish your manuscript too. If you or your colleagues have any manuscript, ready for publication or are working on it, kindly contact us with detailed synopsis and the list of contents. We would transform your work, into a valuable publication. If you wish, we can also suggest you, the suitable subjects for writing books, related to your area of expertise. Manas is known for its publishing quality and commitments. We take utmost care in production and give wide publicity to the book, as well as its author, through our national and international distribution network.

Unmasking Kashmir

A Bureaucrat Reveals

Sonali Kumar, IAS
(Jammu & Kashmir Cadre)

Edited by
Prasenjeet Kumar

Manas Publications
(We Convert Fighters into Writers)
New Delhi-110002 (INDIA)

MANAS PUBLICATIONS

(We convert Fighters into Writers)

(Publishers, Distributors, Importers & Exporters)
4402/5-A, Ansari Road (Opp. HDFC Bank)
Darya Ganj, New Delhi-110 002 (India)
Off. 23260783, 23265523, Res. 23842660
Fax: 011-23272766
E-mail: manaspublications@gmail.com
manaspublications@yahoo.com

Website: www.manaspublications.in

ISBN 978-81-7049-537-6
₹ 695/-

Designed at Innovative Processors

Printed in India at
R.K. Print Services, Delhi and
Published by Mrs Suman Lata for
Manas Publications, 4402/5-A, Ansari Road (Opp. HDFC Bank),
Darya Ganj, New Delhi-110 002 (INDIA)

Disclaimer

This book reflects the author's present recollection and experiences over time. The conversations in the book are not written to represent word-for-word transcripts. Rather, the author has retold them in a way that evokes the feeling and meaning what was said and in all instances, the essence of the dialogue is accurate.

In the event that narrations hurt the feelings of any person, living or dead, or of any group or community, or appear to damage their reputation, the author assures that it has been never her intention to deliberately cause any such hurt or damage and that the same is unintended and unintentional.

Although the author has made effort to ensure that the information in this book was correct at press time, the author does not assume and hereby disclaims any liability to any party for any loss, damage, or disruption caused by errors or omissions, whether such errors or omissions result from negligence, accident, or any other cause.

"Until the lion learns how to write, every story will glorify the hunter."

African proverb

Dedicated to all those 1000-odd "outsider," "non-state subject," All-India Service officers who have given their best years to the Nation while serving in Jammu & Kashmir.

Contents

Why I Wrote this Book

ANOTHER MEMOIR? Of a bureaucrat?

GROAN... YAWN... Oh No... o... o... o...

What new can you talk of, except of cataloguing the postings you suffered and the "successes" you had over some boring 37-years of service in the government?

What's new about Jammu & Kashmir (J&K) too, when there are so many books already on the subject?

On the Kashmir dispute in the United Nations, on the valour of the Indian Army and how they foiled the "evil designs" of our enemies in 1947, 1962, 1965, 1971 and 1999, on the beauty of Kashmir, about the pilgrimages to Vaishno Devi and Amarnath Shrines and on J&K as a wonderful tourist destination.

And then there are biographies, hagiographies and auto-biographies of politicians *ad nauseam*.

The pain and suffering of the Kashmiri Muslims in those "curfewed nights" of the 1990s have already been catalogued. The Kashmiri Pandits too have written about their horrific exodus, how they lost their little paradise-on-earth, and what is stopping them from regaining that paradise. Agreed.

But what I found missing was—what an outsider Indian Administrative Service (IAS), or for that matter, any officer belonging to any All-India Service (AIS) like IPS (Indian Police Service) or IFoS (Indian Forest Service), goes through while serving in J&K. In my case, there was an added disadvantage—

I was the first outsider lady IAS officer serving my full term in this cadre.

In India, most people have either a love-it-or-hate-it relationship with the IAS. They like it for being the "meritocratic steel frame" that is supposedly keeping the country together. And dislike it for being a "favoured", "twice-born" service that rides roughshod on the aspirations of all other government services in India.

Little do they realise the silent war that most All-India Service officers have to wage against corruption and nepotism in a hostile state "cadre" that is imposed on them for the entire duration of their career. Unlike the Army, Para Military or the Central Services who can escape from any such "bad posting" after a two-year stint.

Willy-nilly, we in the IAS become the nameless faceless bureaucrats who perform the thankless task of holding the country together especially in the North-east and in states like J&K. In J&K, the fight is even more difficult. Because to rampant corruption and nepotism, that every IAS officer is forced to fight everywhere else, is added the deadly ingredients of: communalism, anti-nationalism and, in my case, gender bias.

But what is the big deal I'm making of being an "outsider" in J&K? Aren't about 50% of all IAS officers in every state, by design, "outsiders?"

Well, the difference is that unlike any other state, in J&K, an "outsider" or a "non-state subject" can't buy property, can't educate her children in any technical—medical or engineering college, can't get her spouse or children to find employment with the State Government, can neither vote in nor stand for any state-level elections even after retirement, can't even get her son married to a local girl because that will immediately extinguish that girl's *state-subject* status, and so on.

And why? Because a law passed by the Maharaja of J&K in 1927 (20 years before India became independent and J&K acceded to India) says so. The law was enacted by Maharaja's Hindu advisors primarily to keep other Hindus of India out of

J&K. And the same law is now coming in handy for Kashmiri Muslims to keep everyone else out!

But what happens to the Indian Constitution and my (and those girls' who have committed the cardinal sin of marrying non-state subjects) fundamental right to property, employment or franchise?

Shhhhh... Don't even talk about it, lest you upset the fragile Hindu-Muslim amity in the country.

Okay, so let the Government of India then look after the interests of these All-India Service officers by letting them to come to Delhi (or whichever place in India they belong to) to construct their homes, to look after their old parents who can't do "durbar move" in the sunset of their lives in J&K, to let their children study or to find employment for them...?

Hah, are you in your right senses?

Government of India instead loves dragging back to J&K even those All-India Service officers who may have with proper permission come to Delhi (or to whichever place in India they belong to) for any of those normal human needs.

And what happens to their service interests when they get back to J&K? Are they allowed to hold the cadre posts that are meant to be manned by them under rules made by the same Government of India? Do they get their latest Pay Commission or even Dearness Allowance benefits announced by the same Government of India when their compatriots elsewhere get it? Are their seniorities protected under rules made by the same Government of India? Do they get their pensionary benefits in routine as their batch mates get it elsewhere without fighting for it every inch of the way? Can they hope to get official accommodation in J&K the same way as they get while they are with the Government of India?

Now, you are rocking the boat too much!!! You need to be taught a lesson you will never forget.

So that's the CURSE of being an "outsider" in J&K I'm talking about.

But what about the curses of that "outsider" to J&K? Are you sure the present problems are ONLY communal, i.e. how can the Muslims in J&K live with a Hindu India? Or instigated by Pakistan? Or because of the Kashmiri's genuine desire to separate from India?

And NOT because of those tears of the "outsider," shed while serving as bonded labour in J&K?

Just think about it!

On a side note, many people speak about the bureaucratic hurdles they face in their everyday lives. Funnily, whether it is water, electricity, telephones, or any other thing, they always blame the IAS for all ills. Not even knowing whether IAS is indeed responsible for it or not.

Little did I realise that my entire career would be a fight against bureaucratic hurdles where my being in the IAS wouldn't matter. But then, that was because I was in J&K, which as you would have guessed by now, is on another planet.

I have worked in the J&K cadre for 36 and a half years and have spent another year watching events unfold as Arun, my husband, was still in the IAS there. This experience of 37 and a half years is something I thought I needed to share in this background.

For me, writing this book was a cathartic experience where all my pent-up feelings could finally find some expression. I expect little, but only hope this book proves useful both in understanding what the IAS does in J&K and in helping frame some national policies for dealing with the problems there.

Chapter 1

Meeting Sheikh Abdullah

THE TWO-HOUR journey from Baramulla to the Civil Secretariat in Srinagar, rattling over some 54 kilometres (km) of potholed road, was by now a daily affair for me. Among my companions in the bus that day in July 1980 were two smelly sheep and a couple of live chicken in the hands of a freckled youngster.

A wizened old woman was sitting on the floor carrying a plastic bag containing a few live fishes in some water. I must be looking quite strange in a formal silk *saree* and *bindi* (the round sticker that some Indian women sport on their foreheads) but no one seemed to mind.

The journey was important because we were to meet Sheikh Mohammad Abdullah, the legendary Chief Minister of Jammu and Kashmir that day. He had to decide whether I should be allowed to join the Indian Administrative Service (IAS) cadre of Jammu and Kashmir (J&K) state or not.

But am I not getting ahead of myself? So, let me start from the beginning.

Making it to the IAS

1979 WAS THE year when it looked like all my dreams were coming true. I still remember the scent of the letter, the letter of my dreams, I was holding in my hands. The letter that proudly announced to the world that I had made it.

Like my father, I wanted to be an Indian Administrative Service (IAS) officer, supposedly the *crème de la crème* of government administration in India. Being a girl, whenever I talked about my dreams with anyone, I had to face sniggers, and even downright hostility. In Patna, my home town, a girl wasn't supposed to dream of becoming an IAS officer. Instead, she was supposed to sit at home, cook meals, take care of her husband and *children and* accept fate as it is.

"To become an IAS officer, you need to have the lady luck smiling at you," I was told.

"And how do you know the lady luck won't be smiling at me?" would often be my irreverent, irritated retort.

I had earned the reputation of being a girl who was too *ambitious*. Waaayyyyyyy too ambitious!

Making it to the IAS wasn't easy. It meant competing with around 300,000 candidates from all over India. Just for 100-odd seats. It meant proving those people wrong who believed my dreams would never come true. And above all, it meant believing in myself.

On 11 July 1979, I landed up in Mussourie, at the *Lal Bahadur Shastri National Academy of Administration*—the name of the academy was as long as a sentence—for the start of my mandatory two-years of training. Mussourie was a breathtakingly picturesque, mist-laden, British-era hill station of the then-Uttar Pradesh. But that is only one part of the story.

It was in Mussourie, I met the man of my dreams. What can I tell you about him? He was... a little snooty at first, more interested in his camera than me. He was dreamy, charming, funny though sarcastic at times, but above all my best friend. He was somewhat like Mr. Darcy in "Pride and Prejudice" that I read during my English literature days. He was a real cutie pie, and I fell in love with all his qualities—*especially* with his imperfections. And we soon decided to get married.

In a classic tale of romance, if the couple gets married at the end, it is a happily ever after story. But if the couple marries in the beginning, then you expect conflict. Forces trying to tear the lovers apart. And keeping you on tenterhooks on whether the lovers will remain together or be separated forever?

My story, like a typical romance novel, wasn't any different. I have already told you that we decided to get married in the beginning. Then... then what?

No dream lasts forever, and I didn't realise that my dream was soon going to come crashing down. Real hard.

It was time for cadre allotment. *Oops what that was?*

Cadre allotment was something like... Hogwarts Houses in Harry Potter. To which House will you go—Slytherin, Gryffindor, Hufflepuff or Ravenclaw—each with its own merit and its own set of problems. Except that there were more Houses or States here—over twenty-five.

This was a strange practice reserved only for the All-India Services like the IAS where you are allotted a state (also called cadre, which was confusing for all sort of reasons) for the entire duration of your career. Which somewhat sounds like life imprisonment, isn't it?

India is a land of diverse cultures, languages and traditions. And we were soon going to find out that first-hand. There are 18 official languages and hundreds of local languages and customs. Being allotted to a state in the IAS meant you had to learn the language and the local laws and the customs of that state. You had to work there for a couple of years (nine being the minimum). Then come to the Centre, that is the Government of India (GOI), once in a while, if you so wish, and if the GOI agrees to accept you. Then go back to your state again, and repeat the process, if you have the stamina to do that.

Confusing, right? But the bottom line remains that you have to spend most of your career in the state you are allotted to and any time spent OUTSIDE that state has to be *agreed to by that state.* Which somewhat sounds like you can be let out on parole only once in a while!

So for all practical purposes the great IAS actually becomes a bonded labour of some State Government!

The practice, strange and cruel as it may sound to some, didn't worry me too much because till then, there was an unstated convention that lady officers would be posted as close to their homes as possible. Which meant that I would be posted either in my home state Bihar or a state close to Bihar. Hopefully.

Plus, I had also noticed many officers calling their cadre state as their "home." For example, in Bihar (where my father also served as an IAS officer), I had noticed how some Tamilian officers had comfortably settled down in their own houses in Patna after their retirement. So, cadre allotment couldn't be that scary, I thought!

But when the dreaded list was finally pinned on the notice board, it was mayhem all-around.

Horrors! Horrors! Our worst nightmares had indeed come true. Padmini from Tamilnadu was allotted Haryana. Kusumjit from Punjab was given Nagaland. And I from Bihar was allotted Kerala.

It was really like... the Sorting Hat (sorry, Harry Potter wasn't born then!) had made all the decisions for us. And we felt like we had been "hufflepuffed."

I want Bihar; no sorry baby since you said Bihar I'm going to post you as far south as possible. To Kerala. To keep our country united and integrated!

I could hear the Sorting Hat laughing in my ears.

There were obviously some big, misogynistic forces in the Home Ministry throwing us lady officers all- around India in some misguided attempt at National Integration!

Arun, my husband, was allotted Jammu and Kashmir (J&K), because he had fallen in love with its snow-covered mountains after a 14-day trek. The Sorting Hat had fulfilled his wish. And denied mine!

So here was the biggest conflict at the heart of our romantic story. Arun to J&K, I to Kerala. It was like Arun had been posted to Mercury and I to Pluto. Or may be to some other galaxy.

As my US-based brother remarked, if distance could make the heart grow fonder, we couldn't have been posted further apart!

I desperately wanted a "cadre change." So, we moved an application in the Academy itself but we didn't indicate where we wanted to go—J&K, Kerala or a third state. Actually, at that time... we didn't know... where we wanted to go.

So, we decided we should go to our respective states first, compare notes and then decide where we should head for, finally.

That is how Arun landed up in Baramulla in North Kashmir while I was posted as the Assistant Commissioner Training, Trivandrum, Kerala.

Landing up in Kerala

THE JOURNEY TO Trivandrum from my home town Patna, Bihar was... exhausting, in all senses of the term. I had to go first to Kolkata (then-Calcutta) by train. From there, I took another train to Chennai (then-Madras) and then a third train from Madras to Trivandrum. It took over 72 hours in all! It felt like travelling around the world in 72 days! (*oops* sorry 72 hours I mean).

I was homesick even before I had reached Kerala! My 23-year-old mind calculated that if I had to go home on leave ever, it would take me a minimum of 3 days, each way. Which meant six days of travelling for a week's leave. In other words, if I took one week's leave, I'd be in Patna for only one day!

Unknowingly, I had awakened the curse of the "outsider" in the All-India Services which no "insider" allotted to his home state (i.e. a Malyali allotted to Kerala or a Punjabi allotted to Punjab) need ever experience.

Today Kerala is a tourist destination—touted as God's own country. But the Kerala of 1980 was a lot difficult, insular and parochial.

My first challenge was the food. My heart longed for whole wheat *atta rotis* which no Malyali could arrange for me.

Next, I would wish for any curry—mutton, chicken, fish or veggie—cooked in pure mustard oil. But no. Malyalis in those days used *coconut oil* for cooking, which sadly till then I had used only in my hair! I couldn't stomach that smell at all. That very smell that used to come from my hair! Can you imagine your food smelling like your hair?

I couldn't have any of my favourite vegetables like cauliflower or cabbage because these just couldn't be grown in tropical Kerala in those days.

The state had a dominant trade union culture in which strange creatures like IAS officers were considered an *unnecessary irritant*.

Once I asked my office orderly to get me some bread, which he did. But thereafter, the chap didn't attend office for the next 3 days.

On the 4th day, when he turned up, I asked him, "What happened? Were you not well? Where were you for 3 days?"

"No, I took leave," he said in a heavy Malayali accent. His tone was unapologetic.

"Leave? Why?"

"Yesterday you'd asked me to buy some bread. PERSONAL work." Now his heavy accent felt like he was almost singing.

I was dumbstruck. This chap took 3 days of unauthorised leave because I had the temerity of asking him to do a PERSONAL work, which was to get me a loaf of bread which I couldn't find myself!

I was more amused than angry.

Kerala was full of many horror stories. Stories like many officers coming out of meetings after 1730 only to find that their drivers had called it a day exactly at 1730 hours when the offices close officially! This was indeed God's own country.

Anyway, I'm not saying I hated my job. I loved it. Nor am I complaining about Kerala. The memories I have of the place make me laugh even till this day. I enjoyed meeting new people and so many cartoon characters! Characters that became the butt of my jokes at almost every dinner party I attended. Even till this day.

But what was eating me alive—was my distance from Arun. Whenever I had spare time, I wrote letters to him. These were the days with no mobile phones or e-mails. We had no access to land lines either. So, letters were our only way of communicating with each other.

I had a lot to write. Too many stories and emotions to share. I started writing a few sentences and realised that I soon ran out of paper. Soon I was writing as many as five letters daily. Arun did the same.

We shared our sorrows and joys, experiences of places and people. I always imagined how Arun would be feeling up in the mountains. And I'm sure he too was doing the same about me dumped in the sea!

But no matter how much I wrote, I always fell short of words. I wanted to... express my emotions but the space on paper was always limited. I wanted instant communication. I wanted to see him in person. Speak to him all day.

And no! Modern day technology like mobile phones or Skype or whatever does not make things any better if that's what you were thinking.

There were many IAS couples who were posted in different states. Husband in one, wife in another. They met each other a couple of times in a *year*. And *shockingly*, some seemed to be fine with it.

But for me, as time passed, the separation became more and more painful. I was enjoying my job, but I was... alone.

Whenever I received a letter from Arun, my heart jumped with joy. I stared at his hand-writing for hours. His hand-writing was the only real thing I had.

I was glad to know he was happy in Baramulla. He was staying in one of the VVIP suites in the Dak Bungalow. He described the view of the snow-covered hills which I thought was quite exotic. There were 50 apple trees in full bloom just behind his room.

The way he worded his letters, I knew how much he missed me. I wished I was there watching the apple orchards in the backdrop of snow-covered peaks with him.

I was also glad to know Arun was getting all kinds of winter vegetables (like cauliflower and cabbage—my favourite). These were also cooked in mustard oil (my favourite cooking oil), in routine, with no fuss. As for going home, it was just an 18-hour straight journey by Himgiri Express from Jammu compared to travelling around the world in 72 hours that I had to endure.

Like my husband, I too enjoyed the fresh cool breeze of the mountains, lush green valleys and snow-covered peaks. I hated the hot Indian summer, which would make my father chuckle.

"My daughter belongs to the mountains," he would say.

And it was soon going to be true.

By sharing letters, it became clear that I was better off going to J&K than Arun coming to Kerala.

Arun moved an application to the J&K Government for getting me over. I had to get the Kerala Government to agree to spare me, which to be fair to them, they did pretty reluctantly. Some of my seniors there, who knew something about J&K, cautioned me.

"J&K does not have much off an IAS cadre or culture," they said in their typical bureaucratic way. I think what they meant was—I was making a terrible mistake, a mistake I would regret soon!

But I was unrelenting, primarily because I didn't know what they meant!

One and a half months passed.

There was no news, negative or positive, from the J&K Government. The silence was eerie.

Telephones being what they were, we kept writing 4-5 letters a day. We exchanged notes on the merits or otherwise of moving to J&K.

Till I decided enough was enough.

Getting my Cadre Changed to J&K

SO TOTALLY ON a whim, I applied for leave and decided to go to J&K. I had to go to Delhi first by train and then to Jammu. Arun came to Jammu, two days' journey from Baramulla, to pick me up from the Railway station. It was refreshing to find that he looked the same, *sans* beard or moustache.

Next day we took a local bus to first Srinagar, the summer capital of J&K, which was about 300 kms. and then another one to Baramulla, about 54 kms. away.

The beauty of Kashmir in 1980 was just "awesome," as my nephews staying in US would proclaim. The mesmerising journey to Baramulla with tall poplar trees on both sides of the road reminded me of so many Hindi film songs that were shot on that stretch. Like *jane mera dil kise dhoond raha hai, in hari bhari wadiyon me* (I don't know who my heart is looking for in these green verdant valleys).

The bus dropped us on the main road from where we dragged our luggage to the PWD Dak Bungalow where Arun was staying.

This was a quaint building with a sloping tin roof and just four rooms. One VVIP room no. 1 was permanently reserved for state dignitaries like the Chief Minister. Arun had managed the other semi-VVIP room no. 4. And yes, the huge lawn in front and the 50 apple trees in bloom behind was exactly the way I had imagined from Arun's letters.

The cook Akbar Khan, with his flowing white beard, and the butler Fateh Butt, despite his lack of vision in his right eye, were effusive in their welcome. Both were above 60 years in age but Arun had cautioned me NOT to comment on that "sensitive issue" as the age of retirement from government service then was 58. Later I learnt that Fateh Butt's son, who worked in some department, had already retired from the government! That made Fateh Butt above 70 years but I kept my maths to myself.

Akbar Khan, the cook, had cooked two mutton curries in my honour, one *Rogan Josh* (the red curry) and another *Yakhni* (the white yoghurt based curry). And yes, both were cooked in *mustard oil* and were delicious.

Later I learnt that for all our meals they were *billing* Arun his *entire salary* for the month! Anyway, I still felt so welcome that I immediately fell in love with Kashmir and its people.

Next morning, we took a bus to the secretariat in Srinagar. We met Mr. BN Safaya, the suave, aquiline nosed, Secretary GAD (General Administration Department) who was courtesy incarnate. And then we called on the Chief Secretary, Mr. Noor Mohammad.

Mr. Noor Mohammad was one of the most influential men in the whole of J&K. In our little research, we had discovered that Mr. Noor Mohammad had started his service as a *junior stenographer* in the legislative assembly (without coming through any transparent recruitment process). First shock!

Later through his "connections," he had managed to get promoted to the IAS with a funny seniority of 1956 and a half. He could thereafter hold all senior posts under the State Government with ease. And now he was the Chief Secretary or the topmost bureaucrat in J&K. This made him somewhat like Jaffar in Aladdin, the evil sorcerer who could keep the Sultan under his control by casting a spell.

Mr. Noor Mohammad was definitely a dodgy man, as we would soon learn.

Unlike Mr. Safaya, Mr. Noor Mohammad didn't at all look like a "Kashmiri." He was short, fat and surprisingly as dark as a Bihari... like Arun, as I joked. But he spoke English with a clipped non-Kashmiri accent and floored us with his expansive mannerism welcoming us to J&K with open arms, literally.

My heart leapt with joy. I mistook his mannerisms to mean that *our cadre change to J&K shouldn't be a problem.* With this contented feeling, we returned to Baramulla.

We were soon to realise how wrong we were.

A week passed and nothing happened. No news! Nothing!

I decided to venture back to Srinagar. Arun was engrossed in his work, so it was not possible for him to join me.

Like a brave warrior, I hopped on to a bus to Srinagar. Which meant enduring a 2-hour bone rattling journey on horrible roads on a rickety bus to the Batmaloo bus stand. And then *walking* 2 kilometres (yes, *walking*) to get to the secretariat. And being stopped by security guards at the gate as if I was the biggest criminal walking to the secretariat. Well, for a while, I did feel like a criminal.

"I am an IAS probationer," I would squeak.

The guard would look surprised. *How can a lady be an IAS officer?* After all, till then, there was only one other lady IAS officer in the state. She was a local from Jammu *and* 10 years my senior. Also, IAS officers don't enter the secretariat on foot, do they?

Once inside, I was repeatedly told that I had no chance of getting "accepted" in J&K.

Why? Because no "outsider" had ever been taken in "by choice" by the State Government. All "outsider" officers, in fact, advised me to do a favour to my husband by taking him to some other state to escape this virtual prison.

My heart sank when I heard the word *outsider* for the first time. How could I be an *outsider* in my own country? I was an *Indian* first and then anything else. Little did I realise then that the entire Kashmir problem was because of the apartheid regime that existed. That regime which divided humanity into two: *insiders* and *outsiders.*

Being the stubborn person I am, the more I heard those negative comments, the more determined I became to come to

J&K. After all, isn't this state a part of India and am I not in THE INDIAN Administrative Service?

The travel to Srinagar became a daily grind. Which meant enduring a 2-hour bone rattling journey on horrible roads on a rickety bus. And then *walking* 2 kilometres (yes, *walking*) to the secretariat from the bus stand. And being stopped by security guards at the gate as if I was the biggest criminal walking to the secretariat. And then watching the security guards make a strange face as if they had never seen a woman IAS officer. In their whole lives.

Every day my struggles were increasing in intensity. I was entitled to only a month of leave which was finishing fast. Time was running out. If I wasn't accepted in J&K, I would be forced to go back to Kerela.

Finally, Mr. Safaya, the Secretary GAD, took pity on me and told me there was NO possibility of my being accepted in J&K.

"But why?" I was incredulous.

"The State Government had just issued an order creating a parallel cadre to the IAS up to the rank of the Additional Chief Secretary. So, they would be soon replacing the IAS with the local cadre KAS."

What Mr. Safaya, the Secretary GAD, said in a typical bureaucratic language made no sense. What he meant was: That the IAS (a national service) will soon be replaced by a local KAS (Kashmir Administrative Service) and then we can kick you *outsiders* out of our beloved state.

This would be the first step towards getting more *autonomy* for the state. And, of course, Mr. Noor Mohammad, the Chief Secretary (and the evil sorcerer!), was the chief architect of this idea.

So, I was told to forget my dream of getting accepted into J&K. Mr. Noor Mohammad would never agree to that.

Which made us even more stubborn. Instead of giving up, we decided to go up the next level, to the Chief Minister (CM).

The same afternoon, we *walked* four kilometres. Yes, I am

emphasising on *"walked."* To the CM's house behind Nedou's Hotel on the Maulana Azad Road. We were confronted by a balding, pot-bellied, private secretary, who looked us up and down and decided that we were too *lowly* to deserve an audience with the Honourable CM.

So, we were back to the secretariat the next day. There we bumped in to Mr. Mohammad Yousuf Dar, an about-to-be-promoted IAS officer from Kashmir. We had met Mr. Dar in Mussourie where he had come for compulsory training like all of us. For some strange reason, he had got along well with Arun who was half his age.

Taking pity on us, Mr. Dar explained, rather patiently, that we should have actually tried to see the Secretary to CM who was *different* from the private secretary to CM. The latter was there to just take dictations and type out letters while the former advised on files and other weightier issues. Routine appointments were certainly handled by the private secretary but the more important engagements invariably went through the Secretary.

It was all so confusing!

So, we had to focus on meeting the Secretary to CM, Mr. Ghulam Ahmad, a promoted IAS officer. That took another day.

Mr. Ahmad was a suave, well-dressed officer belonging to the Kashmir valley who gave us a patient hearing and then said:

"Yours is a *sensitive* case. What I can do is simply to get you to meet the CM. But I must warn you that I cannot promise any positive outcome. The CM has a mind of his own. So, this would be your first and last chance to impress him."

We nodded. My mind was stuck on the word *sensitive.*

And this is how we came to meet the great Sheikh.

Sheikh Muhammad Abdullah, popularly known as Sher-i-Kashmir was a legend in his lifetime. For some people, he was a charismatic politician who had fought for Kashmir's independence/autonomy all his life. For others, he was a traitor because he had once connived with the Americans to declare independence for Kashmir. For some, he was a saint, a *Pir Baba*, who had miraculous powers to heal the sick.

For us, Sheikh Abdullah was something else. He was the one and the only one to decide—the fate of our quest for being together in J&K.

The D-day had come, and we were ushered to the 3rd floor official chambers of the CM in the Srinagar Secretariat. I still remember the smell of wood polish and the sight of the intricate wood carvings inside his office.

The smell created a mild panic attack. *What if Sheikh Abdullah said no? What would happen then?* My heart had reached my mouth. My mind was coming up with all kinds of horrible, *what if,* scenarios.

We entered the room. And had our first "darshan" of the great Sheikh dressed in a cream achkan with a red rose in his right breast pocket. Quite like the way his friend Jawaharlal Nehru, the first Prime Minister of India, used to dress up. He looked quite charming and elegant.

We introduced ourselves and started explaining. Sheikh Sahib immediately put us at ease by asking us the usual questions: where we were from, where and what did we study, etc.

Since I do talk a lot, as I have generally been accused of (!), and since I was THE OUTSIDER trying to come to J&K, I was soon blabbering non-stop. I feared I had spoken too much. When suddenly Sheikh Sahib lifted his hand, and cut me off. *Was he angry? Annoyed? Or irritated by what I said?*

Instead what I heard was,

"You know I really like officers like you. But I don't know why Government of India only sends me junk."

I was too flabbergasted to say anything, except, "But Sir, I do want to come here."

Sheikh Abdullah's eyes lit up, "Then what's the problem?"

I told him that the Chief Secretary (Mr. Noor Mohammad, the evil sorcerer) probably had some "reservations."

Sheikh Sahib pressed the buzzer and called for my file. The file was produced within five minutes.

Ignoring the six-page comments of the Chief Secretary, Sheikh Abdullah just scrawled two lines in his big, bold handwriting:

"The CS should reconsider his stand and send a telex today to Delhi conveying our concurrence."

The CM then turned towards us and said with a twinkle in his eyes,

"And remember, I'm not as *nikamma* (incompetent) as the Government of India that sends husband to Kashmir and wife to Kerala. I understand the language of the heart. I promise that I'd always post you together."

Bewildered, we stood up and bowed.

And that's how my adventures in J&K began.

Chapter 2

Bumbling about in Baramulla

SHEIKH ABDULLAH remained true to his promise. My cadre change was soon cleared by the Government of India, and I was formally *accepted* into J&K. The State Government also ordered me to complete my training with Arun in Baramulla.

Arun was then reporting to Mr. Shams-ud-Din, the Deputy Commissioner (DC) of Baramulla. The latter treated us with kindness and respect. Once he even took Arun along (when my formal orders had yet to come) to a *stone pelting* episode on the lone bridge on River Jhelum.

This was the first time Arun had seen what a stone pelting episode looked like. And this wasn't 2017. This was 1980 when supposedly peace prevailed in the Kashmir valley.

The old city was across the brown Jhelum River. The houses seemed like they were built on each other or so close to each other as if they were hugging each other.

Arun saw a procession coming out on the narrow streets of the old city. They were carrying the Pakistan flag and shouting slogans in favour of Pakistan. They were all men, bearded and looked like clones of each other.

Jeev-e-jeeve-e-Pakistan
Jeev-e-jeeve-e-Pakistan
Jeev-e-jeeve-e-Pakistan

Which meant long live Pakistan as if Pakistan was a dying nation!

People were clapping, and the slogans were in a nice rhythm. Arun was horrified. In no other part of India, had he seen people shouting slogans to support Pakistan.

The whole damn thing didn't stop there. The crowd suddenly turned violent and started throwing stones at… everyone. Vehicles, tourist buses, police Jeeps—it didn't matter.

Mirwaiz Maulana Farooq (no, not the current Mirwaiz Umar Farooq but his father) was a diehard opponent of Sheikh Abdullah. He was derisively said to head the "*Bakra*" (Goat) party, because of the beards his radicalised supporters sported. Well, bearded men do look like goats! Sheikh Abdullah, as the *Sher-e-Kashmir* (Lion of Kashmir) was said to head the *Sher* (Lion) party.

So, the fight between the two political adversaries used to be called the "*Sher-Bakra*" fight! Or the lion-lamb fight. Not sure whether the lion always won!

Whatever be the fight, my husband was caught in the cross fire. Arun told me later, how he and the DC were initially ducking the projectiles, as if it were a game of *pithoo* (an Indian street game) where one party tries to hit the other with a rubber ball. The only difference was—there was no rubber ball, and this wasn't a game.

A big stone hit a local policeman fracturing his jaw. Arun realised that stone pelting episodes are not as harmless as some media personalities make them out to be. No wonder in medieval times people could be *stoned* to death.

Anyways to control the mob, Shams Sahib had to order a *lathi* charge and fire in the air, which was technically illegal! That was enough in those days as the demonstrators soon dispersed.

Arun had his first experience of how violent such stone pelting incidents can actually be and we debated for days how these demonstrators could be tackled better.

Kashmiris Alienated? Really???

SHAMS SAHIB once nominated Arun on an interview board to select office clerks, designated as Junior Assistants.

One such interviewee was a highly-qualified fellow with a Master's degree in Statistics.

After the usual rounds of questions, when Arun's turn came, he asked, "Do you know what Article 370 is?"

The guy hesitated, for a few moments. He then gathered his thoughts and started speaking,

"I think that is the provision that empowers the police to shoot at will if there be more than five people together in a public place."

There was pin-drop silence in the room. The guy wasn't some illiterate fellow on the street. He had a Master's degree. And yet he didn't know that Article 370 of the Indian Constitution gives a special status to Jammu & Kashmir? That it promises that no law passed by the Indian Parliament will automatically extend to J&K unless it is adopted by its legislative assembly?

So much so for the alienation of Kashmiris?

Another candidate on being asked to name any other apple producing state in India (apart from J&K) wondered if it could be Punjab!

I wonder if the stone pelting mobs on the streets in Kashmir nowadays would know any better about Article 370 or about the apple growing states of India even today!

Which brings me to an even more disturbing point: if you don't know what your grievances are, or how are you alienated, then you are protesting for what???

Knowing Mr. Wahid

PEOPLE ASK ME, "how is the system unjust to Kashmiris?"

I start with an incident. When I had just received my formal orders for training in Baramulla, Shams Sahib got transferred. He was replaced by Mr. Abdul Wahid.

The problem? Mr. Wahid wasn't an IAS officer. In fact, he was not even in the "Select List" of officers who could be promoted to the IAS any time soon.

Mr. Wahid was posted NOT because he was *capable* but because he was *connected*. So, there you go. A non-IAS fellow was posted to a post specifically meant for the IAS.

Now you may ask: what's the big deal? Why am I creating so much ruckus about it? Am I being a "casteist" who believes that only IAS officers have a God given right to become the Deputy Commissioner (DC) and no one else?

For that, you have to understand how important the post of the DC is in J&K. A DC is not only the District Magistrate but the administrator of the entire district. He looks after everything in the district: law and order, revenue, rural development, water, electricity, roads, schools and so on.

If you dilute this post, you dilute the entire administration at the district level. Which means anything related to development there takes a beating. That's why, in the All-India Services scheme of things, all such posts are identified and "encadred" by the Government of India with the stipulation that such posts are invariably held by an IAS officer.

So, what does an IAS officer brings to the post that a local non-IAS cannot? After all it can be argued that a local understands the problem better than an *outsider*.

One word sums up everything: IMPARTIALITY.

An *outsider* IAS officer is impartial by default. He knows no one. Nor is he *connected*. And a great administrator is one who is *impartial*. A local who is appointed to the same post because he is well *connected* and NOT because he is *capable* can never serve justice to the people of that place. Instead he will always serve his relatives, friends, or some political party with whom he is *connected*.

Without impartiality, justice can never be served to the people of Kashmir.

Noor Mohammad, the then Chief Secretary had begun diluting the All-India Services (which included the IAS, IPS, and IFoS) on a war footing. He had already succeeded in fully supplanting the Indian Forest Service (IFoS) with local officers with the result that NOT a single DFO (District Forest Officer) in 1980 now belonged to the IFoS.

He was working the same way with the Indian Police Service (IPS) and the IAS with almost 50% of all posts of District Superintendents of Police (SPs) and of DCs allotted to non-IPS/non-IAS officers.

His intention was simple: more locals meant greater autonomy to the state. The result was the destruction of the administrative system: where people were selected *not* because of merit but because they were *favourites* of the ruling class or *connected* somehow with the high and mighty of the land.

And when that happens: think how this affects the common Kashmiri?

Coming back to Mr. Wahid, we wondered if our APRs (Annual Performance Reports) written by Mr. Wahid would be valid if on promotion to the IAS he was made junior to us? We also apprehended that if non-cadre officers like him got field posts like that of DCs, what will happen to us when we became eligible for such postings?

Coming back to Mr. Wahid, the new DC (Deputy Commissioner), he had no clue as to what to do with us lowly IAS probationers, and especially two of them. We suspected he even felt threatened by us because one fine morning he suddenly abandoned the traditional DC's office room, the one with bay windows and next to the river Jhelum, and switched that with ours!

I have never before or after heard of a situation where the DC of any district had shifted officially into the room of some trainees. I believe the DC did that because he felt we had lent a certain prestige and aura to the room which he perhaps lacked and which, therefore, had to be taken away from us immediately.

Meanwhile we kept on wondering how Delhi in the DOPT (Department of Personnel and Trainings) was supervising the overall cadre management in J&K. They were the ones laying down rules about cadre posts, stipulating which posts could be held by All-India Officers like the IAS, IPS or IFoS, and which needn't. So, shouldn't they be doing something when those same rules were violated with impunity?

The answer as we later learnt to our bitter chagrin was a resounding NO. No wonder, the practice of putting non-cadre officers on All-India Service cadre posts never stopped and continues even today in J&K in open defiance of whatever the Government of India stipulates.

And there lies one very important part of the "Kashmir Problem."

Visiting Gurez

OKAY, ENOUGH of heavy talk! Let's talk about another of my beautiful experiences in Kashmir.

My peon Juma Lone had been insisting for quite some time that I visit his part of the world—Gurez. A small valley near the Indo-Pak border or as we call it the LOC (Line of control).

I requested the DC, and he allotted us a rickety jeep from the district garages. Gurez was just 100 kilometres from Baramulla. But we took nearly 8 hours as we rattled our way on non-existent roads.

By the time we reached Gurez, it felt like every bone in my body had developed a hairline fracture! No kidding!

Gurez, however, was... an absolutely out-of-the-world experience for us. This valley was separated by high mountain ranges from the Kashmir Valley and connected only for six months through the Razdan Pass.

For the first time in my life, I saw hundreds of the legendary *Bhojpatra* trees on this pass. The white bark of the *Bhojpatra* trees was used for writing in ancient times when paper was still to be invented.

The view from the top of the Razdan Pass was breathtakingly beautiful. Wular lake, the biggest fresh water lake then in

Asia, glittered in the sun like an ocean whose other shore you couldn't see. Thirty-six years later, when I looked at the same water body, I was pained to see it turned in to a pathetic marsh, with paddy fields, poplar and willow plantations and even illegally constructed houses, littering its shores.

We stayed in the Dak Bungalow at Dawar, the Headquarters of Gurez, at an altitude of about 8000 ft. (2600 metres). It was located on the banks of the gurgling Kishanganga River. The view of the hill of Habba Khatoon from the river took our breath away. We fell in love with Gurez immediately.

The wizened old cook at the Dak Bungalow amazed us by rustling up some grilled river trout and caramel custard in our honour. He proudly showed me how he could cook Gurez *Rajmash* (Red Kidney Beans) and chicken without using a pressure cooker even at that high altitude.

The people of Gurez took great pride in distinguishing themselves from Kashmiri although almost all could speak Kashmiri and followed Islam.

"We are not effeminate like the Kashmiris, and we never use *kangris* (the wicker and clay fire-pot that Kashmiris carry inside their loose gowns called *pherans*)" — was the proud refrain we heard wherever we went.

The men were mostly working for the army carrying supplies on mules while the women carried on with agriculture on the small pieces of fertile land they had. Gurez was also famous for its *Shah zeera* (aromatic cumin seeds), *gucchi* (black mushrooms) and lots of rare and expensive medicinal plants.

The warmth and affection of the Gurezies overwhelmed us. Juma Lone, was always by my side, so much so he would not even let me carry my purse.

"No! It's bad manners to carry a lady's purse!" I said when he tried to *snatch* my purse.

"But mam, my whole village will condemn me if I allow my officers to carry their own 'luggage!'"

This... This was the hospitality of the people of Gurez. I was touched.

I also felt a surge of pride that at last somebody was considering me a proper officer.

Juma Lone remains in touch even today.

My First Wazwan

ON OUR RETURN, we learnt that the District SP (Superintendent of Police) had got transferred. The official farewell function was followed by a sumptuous dinner, the kind I had never seen before. This was my first encounter with the famed Kashmiri *Wazwan*, a feast where you are served at least *10* meat dishes, one after the other.

I was the only lady invited as I was the only lady officer serving the district! I soon realised that, unlike Bihar, in Kashmir wives were never invited even for semi-official functions like *farewell parties*.

We sat on the carpet, on the *floor*. Because it was almost winter, we were all given a blanket each to spread on our legs. A bearer then approached us with a portable copper wash basin and another with a jug containing hot water; so, we could all clean our hands without stirring out of our comfortable perches.

Then the food arrived. First to be served was a plate full of boiled rice. Placed atop were three mutton and a chicken dish. While I found others digging into their *seekh kebabs* and *tabaq maaz* (a dry dish made of rib pieces), I was, as I was used to in Bihar, trying to eat these with the rice.

The outgoing SP who was from Jammu realised the mistake that novices like me make while tackling *wazwan* and whispered,

"Sonaliji, rice is only for decoration. Ignore that and focus on the meat only."

I realised what he meant, because even before we had finished the four initial dishes, the curry dishes started being served. There was *rishta*, which was some kind of a meatball cooked in a saffron curry. Then *yakhni*, which was mutton cooked with yoghurt, followed by *roganjosh, aab gosht, dhania korma*… after which I lost count!

Never in my life had I seen or eaten so much of mutton in one sitting. I didn't know how much I was supposed to eat but had learnt that refusing to be served would be insulting the *waza*, or the cook. Then just before I was about to hit the panic button, came a mutton ball cooked in a white yoghurt based curry. This was the *gushtabba*, and as the SP explained, the "full stop" to *wazwan*.

Phew! I heaved a sigh of relief. The whole episode was like a fairy tale. Those goblin-like *wazas*, emerging with huge vessels, in their ash and soot stained white dress, smelling of wood smoke and serving you endlessly. Wow, what a feast.

I looked at my plate and was ashamed how much of rice and other dishes were still left there, untouched. If I had wasted food like this back home in Bihar, I'd have sure been upbraided by my mother. Then I sneaked a glance at the SP's plate and found that in a similar state. That relaxed me a bit.

Anyway, my first encounter with *wazwan* did leave me speechless and stunned.

Meeting Syed Ali Shah Geelani

WE HAD BECOME pretty comfortable with Mr. Wahid, or rather the other way around. He even invited us home for such delicious dishes as mutton cooked with apricots or apple or almonds that we had till that time not even tasted.

It was during one of those rare times of camaraderie that Mr. Wahid took us on a tour to Sopore, the famous Apple Town of Kashmir. There we saw cows gorging on fallen apples and surmised that this was why their milk tasted so sweet!

In the meeting, we met a very interesting man. He was the MLA (Member Legislative Assembly) from Sopore and belonged to the *Jamait-e-Islami* party. I was told by the locals that after Zulfiqar Ali Bhutto, the then-Prime Minister, was hanged by the army in Pakistan, the agitated Kashmiris had beaten up all *Jamait-e-Islami* leaders and had even forcibly shaved off their beards. The local MLA, however, had somehow escaped their wrath because he had gone in to hiding and emerged only when the people were somewhat mollified.

Anyway, at a personal level, the MLA didn't seem obnoxious at all. He spoke to us in chaste Urdu with courtesy and civility.

Except for one stray remark that "too many *outsiders* were nowadays being sent to Kashmir!"

Little did I realise then that this mild-mannered MLA would evolve into the great Syed Ali Shah Geelani, the pro-Pakistani leader of the separatists, constantly spewing venom against India, the country he was still drawing his MLA's pension from!

Apparently Geelani had changed his colours after he started losing elections. This change in strategy ensured that he could be in news even without being an MLA. He could also then be a darling of the intelligence agencies from Pakistan as well as India and milk them both with equal felicity.

Surviving the Kashmir Chill

BY OCTOBER, it was autumn in full bloom. Leaves had turned yellow. The grass had become brown on which frost appeared in the mornings. And Baramulla had become quite chilly.

Our rooms had no modern heaters. Using electric heaters was not an option because the voltage in those days use to drop to as low as 90 volts (as against the mandatory 220 volts)! Power cuts had become frequent as the low water flow in the rivers had reduced the overall electricity generation from all hydro plants in Kashmir. The light bulbs were so dimmed that the joke was that you needed a torch to check whether there was electricity in the house!

Fateh Butt, our room bearer, got us a *wood-fired bukhari* (a tin contraption with a pipe taking the smoke outside the room) that he would load with wood every evening. Once it was lit, we had to put a log in every hour which we did till about 10pm where after we would fall asleep. The fire used to die out by 2 am or so but we were by then so comfortable in our heavy *rajais* (quilts) that cold would hardly bother us.

Villagers would just wrap a heating coil around a wooden block, connect it to the mains and drop that in to the village well to ensure that they got some lukewarm water in the morning. The trick was to take that coil out of the well first thing in the morning, lest someone got electrocuted!

Unable to cope with the rising bills of our meals, I invested in a crude open-coil electric hotplate and a couple of pots, pans and spoons. I was spurred in to making all these "investments" when I once noticed a slice of bread specked with some *green fungus* being served to us.

The explanation? Well, because no one else dined at the Dak Bungalow, the cook could afford to buy only one bread a week for us. That did it and that was the end of ordering our breakfasts from Akbar Khan.

The voltage being what it was, and the rudimentary cooking skills I then possessed, I couldn't go beyond rustling up our breakfasts every day. That was nonetheless a relief because in J&K there used to be NO lunch break in offices. So, in the mornings, we started gorging on two-egg *loaded* omelettes with four toasts and a cup of instant coffee made with condensed milk. Each.

There was no regular milk supply and no fridge to store milk, so condensed milk was the only way out.

During night times (and day times), we heard the sounds of little creatures running across our rooms. Rats!

With the onset of winter, we suddenly found an increase in the population of rats that were literally leaving no stone unturned to enter the warm environs of our room in the Dak Bungalow. Once as we entered the room, Arun saw a big rat with a round face and big round ears and a long tail (he was cute yet scary!) climbing over our thermos flask that was placed on the shelf above the fire place.

Before I could react, Arun had flung the lock that was in his hands at the rat. Surprisingly the lock hit the rat with such force that it killed it instantaneously. In the process, my lone thermos flask was also blown to smithereens!

Our uncharacteristically "violent behaviour," however, didn't deter rats one bit.

Akbar Khan, the cook, had to go to his village in Uri, on the Pakistan border, to attend a wedding. The *baraat* was coming from the Pakistan side, which was commonplace in those days. No one needed a visa or passport. The local army units were cool about such liaisons as the population in the border areas was (and still is) totally with India. Was it because they spoke Pahari and not Kashmiri, we wondered.

When Akbar Khan returned to Baramulla, he presented us with a bag containing about 5 kilos of walnuts. I didn't know what to do with such a "large" quantity. So, we ate a few and put the bag on one of our window sills.

About a fortnight later, when I checked the bag, it was empty. Shocked, I checked here and there but couldn't locate a single walnut in the room. Our first instinct was to suspect that someone had entered our room in our absence and pilfered the whole lot.

But discreet enquiries revealed that no Kashmiri would do that. Why? Because they also didn't know what to do with walnuts, which in any case grew everywhere.

About a month later, around Diwali time, when we wanted our room to be cleaned thoroughly, we shifted the lone sofa in our room. Of course, there was a ton of dirt below the sofa. But what caught our attention was the rattling sound when we shifted the furniture. Curious we looked around and noticed a small hole at the back of the sofa's upholstery.

Fateh Butt, who was helping us around, knew what that meant. Before we could react, he had put the sofa upside down and was shaking it vigorously. To our utter amazement, there tumbled out our lost walnuts. One by one and all five kilos of it. Apparently, a rat family had very laboriously carried these wrapped around their tails and stored them in the sofa as part of their winter stocking mission.

I couldn't take any more chances. So, we immediately deshelled the walnuts, and I turned the kernels in to some kind of sugar *chikkis* (praline). The dish turned out so well that we polished off the lot in about a week.

Soon both of us suffered some peculiar after effects. Arun's tongue swelled up so much that he had difficulty swallowing. I had rashes all over my body.

Our first port of call was the army hospital. There the doctor referred Arun to a dentist and prescribed some ointment for my "skin disease." The dentist concluded that Arun's teeth were so sharp that they had hurt his tongue. So, the remedy was to grind and blunt his teeth somewhat!

Disappointed, we decided to consult Dr. Dar, in the District Hospital, whose reference we had got from our old friend Mr. MY Dar in Srinagar. Dr. Dar had one look and understood the problem.

"Have you had any walnuts recently?"

We nodded and admitted sheepishly that for the past one week we each had about half-a-kilo of walnut *chikki* every day for lunch.

"So that's the culprit!" declared the good doctor. He prescribed us some strong anti-allergic pills. His parting advice was that we don't go overboard on any Kashmiri dish, the wazwan, the *karam saag* (Kale or Chinese Broccoli) or even saffron.

We remembered that advice all our lives!

Celebrating Diwali

BY LATE OCTOBER, Diwali, the festival of lights, was upon us. Diwali has a special place in our Hindu hearts. It is a time for family get-togethers. People would send each other gifts and sweets. All houses would be lit up either with candles or *diyas* or colourful light bulbs. The sound of bursting crackers would be everywhere as if the entire universe had gone into celebration.

This was our first Diwali in Muslim Kashmir. Where no houses were lit up. No gifts were exchanged. No sound of crackers. And we had no friends. Diwali wasn't celebrated at all in Muslim Kashmir, which made us feel lonely. I guess this is how Indians probably feel when they immigrate to the US or the UK.

Anyways, I was with my husband. And for me nothing mattered thereafter.

We still wanted to celebrate Diwali just as it was done in North India. By lighting candles and *diyas* (small earthen pots that are filled with oil and cotton wicks). But we couldn't find any in the local market. Apparently, most of the Hindu population that could celebrate Diwali, was killed or chased away by the Pakistani raiders in 1947.

So, the weekend before we took a trip to Srinagar and bought all the stuff we needed. I also bought a clay figurine depicting Lakshmi, the Goddess of Wealth, who is invoked for showering wealth during this festival.

When we reached Baramulla and opened the packets, we found the figurine of Lakshmi broken. My heart cried. *Why was I so unlucky?* Buying another figurine wasn't easy. We had to go to Srinagar again for that. Which meant a two-hour long journey one way.

We tried to think of an explanation. And couldn't come up with any. The figurine wasn't broken when we bought it. So, we concluded that the jostle in the bus during the journey back was the obvious culprit. I considered that a terrible omen.

Our entire salary was being spent on just paying the bills of the Dak Bungalow. *We were so unfortunate*, I wondered.

Just then, there was a knock on our door. It was Mr. Trishal, the Assistant Commissioner (AC) Revenue. He was carrying a packet in his hands, which he handed over with a cheerful "Happy Diwali!"

When I opened the packet, I was speechless. It contained a framed painting of the Goddess Lakshmi. So, the gods were NOT so angry after all. I thanked Mr. Trishal profusely.

And I carry that image with me even now after 38 years!

***

As darkness fell, we donned our woollens, and ventured out lighting candles and *diyas*. As we finished decorating the windows of our room in the Dak Bungalow, we found an army jeep driving in.

A Colonel in full uniform alighted. He introduced himself as did we.

"I saw the Diwali lights from the main road, and was curious to find out who in Baramaulla, outside army areas, was daring to celebrate Diwali."

We invited him in and served him some *gajar ka halva* (carrot halva) that I had just made.

Colonel Sehgal claimed that it was the best *gajar ka halva* he had ever had in his life and promptly invited us for the special Diwali Dinner that evening in the army mess. We were happy to accept. Anything to reduce our food bills in the Dak Bungalow!

Lakshmi had indeed listened to me. I was after all not alone in Diwali.

***

Over dinner, we bumped in to another IAS officer, some four years our senior. He had driven down from Srinagar for the celebrations. Drinks (which included whisky, beer, rum or wine) and snacks were in abundance and our senior was busy partaking of both. Being teetotallers, we after a glass or two of fruit juice, sneaked out to the river banks for a stroll.

When we came back, our senior looked… drunk. His eyes were bloodshot. He looked at me and burst in to tears.

"*Bhabhi ji* (elder brother's wife), where did you go? I was looking all around for you…" he whimpered.

Bhabhi ji? I couldn't believe my ears, coming as it was from a senior, at least four years older in service and age. Anyway, we all promised that we will now go nowhere.

The senior was somewhat mollified and downed a few drinks more.

By the time dinner was served, the senior couldn't stand on his feet. There was no way he could return to Srinagar that night. Instead, he had to be taken to a guest room in the army mess on a *stretcher*!

The incident shook me and Arun to our bones. We wondered if the indiscretion displayed by that officer was solely the fault of his personality or upbringing? Or was he traumatised because of serving in J&K as an *outsider*? Where you weren't sure when would you get your next promotion or field posting?

Which incidentally our senior was not getting.

***

Our Diwali "celebrations" didn't go unnoticed by the local officer of R&AW (Research & Analysis Wing), the Indian version of the CIA. So, it was his turn next to invite us for dinner. He gave us detailed instructions on how to reach his residence. But we missed a turn and landed in an unfamiliar street.

We stopped a Kashmiri passer-by and described the Sikh officer to enable find his house. The villager had no problem recalling him.

"Oh, that *Khufia* (secret) police Sardarji? Just turn left and his would be the fourth house on the right," he explained.

So much for the secretiveness of the R&AW, we both laughed.

***

In December, we saw our first snow fall. Of the season and of our lives. I used to think that snow was like frozen rain drops. But I was wrong.

I saw snow-flakes falling from the grey sky, soft and pure, gently to the ground. Like a feather. And slowly everything turned white in minutes.

Arun, being the star-photographer of our batch in the Academy, went berserk taking pictures of our snow-covered roof and trees from all angles. But the cold was biting in its intensity and we were glad that our sojourn in chilly Baramulla was coming to an end.

Chapter 3

Escaping to Jammu

AFTER BARAMULLA, we had to move for further training to Jammu where the State Government too had by then moved for the winters. *How peculiar*, I thought. Just because the weather changed, we too like Gujjar-Bakerwals (the nomads) had to shift base.

If you don't know, the Gujjar-Bakerwals take their cattle for grazing in the summer to the highlands and then bring them back to the lowlands. For what? Grazing. We too were moving to the lowlands. For what? I hope not grazing?!

Jokes apart, little did I know then that this bi-annual "shift" from Srinagar to Jammu in November and vice versa in April EVERY YEAR (!) was going to be a constant feature of my life for most of the time we would be in J&K.

But moving to Jammu presented an immediate problem. With the first snowfall, and landslides, the National Highway linking Srinagar to Jammu snapped. There was only one, rather *expensive*, option left. And that was to take a flight out from Srinagar.

So, we got ourselves "relieved" formally from the DC office in Baramulla. And with just our clothes in two small suitcases took a public bus out to Srinagar.

With the good offices of Mr. MY Dar, we had arranged for a room in the MLA's Hostel (yes, in those days, IAS officers in J&K could also stay there!) on the Maulana Azad Road in Srinagar. Dumping our luggage there, we walked over to the

TRC (Tourist Reception Centre) in Srinagar where the office of the-then Indian Airlines was located.

The Monopoly that was Indian Airlines

THESE WERE THE pre-internet days. So, there was no online booking. We had to fill up a form and queue at the counter for what seemed like hours for our tickets. We saw a very bored clerk sitting at the desk as if announcing to the world, *I'm the unhappiest person on earth and I will soon make your life as miserable as possible.*

When our turn came, we handed over the form to her. The clerk glanced over the form and frowned. She then looked up.

"Sorry sir but no tickets are available!"

Funnily she said sorry but her tone was least apologetic and rather indifferent.

We were in a state of panic. *Couldn't travel by road. Cannot travel by air. How else are we going to reach Jammu? Who can help us?*

It was then we remembered dear old Mr. MY Dar, again. Arun called him up and told him about *our* problem.

He listened patiently and then said, "Okay. Why don't you meet the Station Manager of the Airlines? Do it right away!"

We hung up and did the same. And now here was the biggest surprise! Two seats were immediately booked for us for the next day's flight. The clerk had told us that the flight was fully booked?! So then—from where—did two vacant seats emerge suddenly!?

Apparently, the Station Manager had a "quota" for us "senior IAS officers."

Okay, so that was the racket. Keep 60% seats away from the normal public as your private "quota" and then keep on obliging VVIPs as and when they approach you. The trick ensured, as we later learnt, that from the Chief Minister downwards *everyone* knew the Station Manager *personally*.

As for the Station Manager, he had got himself a government accommodation at par with the Chief Secretary (who is the highest-level officer in the state). Not bad at all for a junior employee of a supposedly commercial company!

To cut a long story short, we took the Indian Airlines Avro flight the next day to Jammu. Arun took the window seat and started snapping pictures of the snow-capped mountains with the Avro's propellers whirring in the background. I just closed my eyes to control the discomfort caused by the constantly shaking aircraft.

We survived the first flight of our lives with some Rupees 50 still *left* in our pockets. Despite my cadre change, I still could not get any salary in J&K as my LPC (Last Pay Certificate) from Kerala had yet to reach me.

At the Mercy of Messrs. Tiku and Raina

REACHING JAMMU unfolded a new set of problems. We had no place to live.

Technically, as IAS probationers we were still in training and not entitled to a government house. We couldn't also rent accommodation for just four months because no landlord would agree to that. You either pay rent for the full year or get lost!

We could then only stay in the government Circuit House as we did in Baramulla.

So, we went to the Jammu Circuit House and introduced ourselves as IAS probationers.

"*IAS probationers*, what is that?" asked the House Manager.

We left the little luggage we had at the reception and went to the Secretariat to seek help. We first met Mr. Tiku, the Deputy Secretary Hospitality & Protocol (H&P) and explained *our* problem to him.

"I'm sorry. There is nothing I can do for you!" Mr. Tiku sounded like a typical unhelpful bureaucrat.

There was another young officer sitting in the same room who overheard our conversation. The plate on his table read "Deputy Secretary Tourism."

When Tiku went out of the office room for some time, he moved towards us.

"Hi. I'm Anil Goswami, IAS 1978 batch."

We introduced ourselves.

"I overheard your conversation with Mr. Tiku. Don't worry. I'll help you get a room in the circuit house for one day but..."

We knew the *but* was coming.

"But after that you will be on your own."

Anil rang up someone and we ran back to the circuit house to find a room being miraculously allotted to us. So, we "took possession," shifted our luggage and went for our training.

Two days later, I found a notice lying in my room. It was from the Deputy Secretary Hospitality & Protocol. *Mr. Tiku!* To my horror, it was an eviction notice. We were asked to vacate our room forthwith. I could hear the notice screaming in my ears. GET OUT! GET OUT!

We contacted Anil immediately. He advised us to *ignore* the notice. So, we brazened out and kept on staying till April end (which was for four months) like *shameless homeless* people.

Till we had to move back to Srinagar with the State Government.

***

Another great character we came across was Mr. Raina, the accounts officer of the GAD.

As probationers, we were entitled to travel by bus and NOT by air. Now since we had come by air, because the highway was closed, we could only attach the Indian Airlines ticket with our travelling allowance bill. However, we took care to claim just the bus fare, which we were then entitled to.

Days passed and our bill wasn't cleared. With a pay of Rupees 1100 per month, we were then woefully short of money. We, therefore, went to the accounts officer to enquire.

"Okay. Attach the bus fare with the bill and I'll have it passed," he said.

We were dumbstruck.

"But sir how can we do that since we had to travel by plane?"

"Yes, but how can I pass your bill when you are not entitled to travel by air?"

"But sir that's why we have claimed only the bus fare—"

"Yes, but you have NOT attached the bus ticket!"

We were getting nowhere. So once again, we had to complain to Mr. Safaya, the Secretary GAD, and the accounts officer's *boss*. Needless to add that could immediately get our bill settled.

***

During our training phase, a brilliant idea came to mind.

Why not buy a *scooter* to meet our daily needs? Which will also reduce our dependence on the rather *non-existent* public transport system in J&K in those days?

The most *popular* scooter in those days was the Bajaj Chetak. But for that, you had to be in a *queue* for almost *10 years*!

Tawi Scooters, a public sector undertaking of the J&K Government, was then making a model called Vijay Super. It was available off-the-shelf for around Rupees 7000. The problem was—we could hardly spare Rupees 2000.

We were then undergoing training with the Accountancy Training Institute. Luckily, the Principal of the institute was so impressed with us that he gave us some accountancy manuals to study on our own, and told us not to bother attending his classes!

The manuals taught us—that we could get a *scooter loan* from the *government*. You may ask: why take a loan from the government?

In those days, all banks were nationalised, and they didn't like giving loans for "unproductive assets" like scooters. So, your only option was to get a loan from the government.

Arun applied for a loan of Rupees 5000, which was the maximum permissible amount under rules. The application got stuck with Mr. Raina, the Accounts Officer GAD. Yes, that Mr. Raina with whom we had to move heaven and earth just to get our travel allowance bill cleared.

He rejected our application right away. His reason? That we were still on probation! What???

His logic was that since our services could be terminated with little ado, any loan made to us would put government money at *risk*. In other words, lending to a probationer would be a waste of government money.

So, in his logic, we should wait till we became "permanent" government servants.

Every couple has dreams of owning a house and a car. It wasn't a crime to dream of owning a scooter. But Mr. Raina's logic made us feel like criminals.

Anyways, by then we had become good friends with the Secretary GAD who was Mr. Raina's boss. He used to tell me on my face that he had yet to find someone who had entered J&K against all odds and admired me for my "guts."

During a casual chat, we mentioned our scooter loan problem. He was shocked.

He immediately summoned Mr. Raina and ordered him to put up our file to him right away. Ultimately, the loan for Rupees 5000 was sanctioned, to be recovered over 200 monthly instalments. A big relief!

We took the bank draft to the local seller and returned with our gleaming new scooter.

***

We were also allotted a two-room government flat in Srinagar in an out-of-the-way place called Chhanpora. All thanks to our friend, the Secretary GAD. Yes, it was the end of April. And we were moving back to Srinagar.

Chhanpora was the first place we called *our* HOME. We could now go back to the IAS Academy in Mussourie for our phase-II training. And still come back to this cosy little hole.

It was a place where we could leave our meagre belongings. That included two buckets, an electric hotplate, a frying pan, a pressure cooker, a pot, two plates, four mugs and four glasses. And yes, also the heavy woollens we had acquired to face the cold of Baramulla. Poor *outsiders,* what would we do if we didn't have even this shelter!

***

The time had come to pay our *rent* at the Jammu Circuit House. The bill was... shocking. Because it exceeded our entire salary for six months!

But then we remembered the angel who had saved us earlier in Baramulla from a similar predicament. Parvez Dewan, an IAS officer of 1977 batch of JK cadre, gave us a copy of an old government order that stipulated that IAS probationers while on training had to pay only Rupees 75 every month as room rent (instead of paying Rupees 100 per day or so which was what we were being charged). And an additional Rupees 10 per month for electricity in any government guest house in J&K. This much we could sure afford.

Bolstered, we approached the great Mr. Tiku who *refused* to honour the Government Order.

All our arguments and logic, including that the same order had worked in Baramulla, were just water off a duck's back. First the eviction notice and then this! We had become great enemies with Mr. Tiku. And that too in a matter of months! Wow! We even named his department as the Department of HOSTILITY (instead of Hospitality) and Protocol, but that didn't solve the problem.

Crestfallen, we called on Mr Ghulam Ahmad, the Secretary to CM and also in-charge of the Department of Hospitality and

Protocol. He was the same officer who had earlier helped us meet the CM. He saw our point and honoured the order. Which reduced our bill drastically. He called up Tiku and ordered him rather rudely to let us pay. That was some achievement.

We paid up at the reception. And I met Mr. Tiku for one last time.

This time I refused to call him *Sir*. Instead I told him straight,

"Mr. Tiku. We are leaving the circuit house today, but just pray that you never ever have any official work with me in future."

I had NO idea how would I ever carry out that threat. Nonetheless I felt compelled to communicate my bitterness to him, and that was that.

I noticed a strange thing working in J&K throughout my 37 years of service. There was always a defiance at the lower level to follow laws, rules and orders. I thought this was the case throughout India. But when I spoke to my batch mates elsewhere in India, I realised that this was peculiar only to J&K. Apparently, J&K was never under the British Raj. And hence, there was no concept of rule of law. Even till this day!

So, there you go. Even if law entitled you to something, you would always be denied that. Until you could move a higher court of appeal!

Chapter 4

Surviving my First Posting

BACK FROM OUR Phase-II training at Mussourie, we were just taking it easy in Srinagar. In those days, it took months to get your first posting. So instead of worrying, we decided to travel throughout Kashmir to keep ourselves busy.

With a brand new scooter in our possession, we were soon off to the beautiful Sonemarg one day, Yusmarg the other, and so on and really enjoying our *paid holiday*. The freedom from the rickety (and smelly) public transport was unbelievable.

But the fun was short-lived. Just a week later, while filling up at a petrol pump, we learnt that our postings had come. I was to go as Deputy Secretary Agriculture and Arun as Deputy Secretary Power Development Department.

There were NO field postings i.e. as Sub-Divisional Magistrates (SDM-one rung below DC) for us. Because, as we guessed, Mr. Noor Mohammed, the Chief Secretary was still too angry with us. Then we learnt of his attempts to post 1977 batch IAS officers (like Madhav Lal and Parvez Dewan) as first Naib-Tehsildars (two rungs below SDM) and when they protested as Tehsildars (one rung below SDM).

Noor Mohammad was doing this deliberately to bring IAS officers at par with the local KAS (Kashmir Administrative Service) officers. Anyway, when too much pressure was put on him by the Central Government, he very reluctantly posted the 1977 batch officers as Sub-Divisional Magistrates, which was what they were entitled to in the first place.

The subsequent batch i.e. 1978 also got sub-divisions in routine, but after a delay of three months, which left quite a bad taste in the mouth. But when our turn came, Noor Mohammad was hell bent to deny us any field postings.

In fact, he used to declare openly that he hated the thought of young IAS officers "lording like little viceroys" in their sub-divisions. Otherwise too, unlike any other state, J&K is not 'naturally' divided into districts and sub-divisions. So, some sub-divisions (which were just Tehsils) in far flung or trouble prone areas like Zanskar, Bhaderwah, or Basholi were created artificially just to 'accommodate' (and actually punish) young IAS officers.

You've been very bad boys; so I'm going to send you to a boarding school in Baghdad!

There was no option for us but to join our secretariat postings. But when I walked into the secretariat, I was stunned to discover that I had been allotted a room with seven other under-secretary level officers. IN THE SAME ROOM! This never happened in the Government of India where Deputy Secretaries generally had an independent room for themselves.

Not that I minded social interaction with my juniors. But... what bothered me the most was: I had deliberately not been allotted an independent room for myself because I had to be *shown* my place. As an *outsider*.

So much for cracking the IAS examination, I sighed!

Anyway, I had come to J&K "by choice," as my seniors never failed to rub it in. So, there was no option but to grin and bear it.

Worse was yet to come. I was given NO work. Sheikh Ghulam Rasool, the Agriculture Secretary, was firmly in Mr. Noor Mohammad's camp and believed he could *chase away* young IAS officers faster (to Delhi or wherever!) by insulting them.

So, to kill time, I read up the annual reports, the departmental publications, the statistical handbooks, anything

I could lay my hands on. And when that was not enough, I started reading all the books on Kashmir available in the secretariat library. We even arranged with a local bookseller to borrow and return one magazine every day by paying him a Rupee per magazine.

Experiencing my First "Durbar Move"

THEN CAME OCTOBER, and it was time for the great Durbar to move to Jammu. Now in Srinagar, as I mentioned, we had a small flat which we could call our own. But lo and behold, when we reached Jammu, we were allotted just one-room in the Tourist Reception Centre—with no kitchen, no pantry, Nothing!!! Just one-room with an attached bathroom—that's all!

We hated eating out all the time. Our mouths craved for a home cooked meal. In Srinagar, we had our own HOME and a small kitchen where we could cook our meals. Now here we come to Jammu. And are stuffed in one-room WITHOUT A KITCHEN. Let me say that again.

You can imagine what cooking would be like in a single room?! A real nightmare! I remember one evening I made rice and wanted to strain the hot water after it was cooked.

I looked here and there and found no such place to strain the water. My eyes then fell onto the small balcony outside our room. *This is it! Let me drain the water from this small balcony,* I thought.

I moved to the balcony and began draining the water. I heard a volley of abuses after that! *What had I done wrong???*

It was then I realised that the hot water had dripped on someone's head below. Which obviously made him scream. Stunned, I had to learn soon how to make rice, without straining. The solution??? Use a pressure cooker instead, stupid!

Looking for a House in Jammu

ANYWAY, TO CUT a long story short, I still needed a place to live like a normal human being. Many other IAS officers, including some seniors, were allotted a similar one-room accommodation in the same building but they were lumping it in rather stoically.

When I questioned them point blank, they admitted that they had to, like good Hindus, suffer because of their *bad karmas*!

I didn't think I had earned any bad *karmas*. Or even knew what was in store in my destiny. So, I suggested that we all go together and bring our plight to the notice of the CM and the Governor. NO ONE AGREED.

If people are so convinced that they have to suffer, nothing can be done about it.

But I wasn't the one to give up so easily. So, we went to the Gandhinagar government colony. And found out that at my level I was *entitled* to a "B type" house. Read it as a B-grade house. Or rather C-grade. The houses from the outside looked as if they were about to crumble. Plaster was peeling off due to seepage. And the wall and roofs of many houses had become green because of algae!

Anyways, I needed a house then. And a B-grade house was still better than no house!

Making friends with the *chowkidar*, I made out a list of all those who were staying in "B grade" houses. I noticed that some of the houses were allotted in the names of *officers* or *politicians* who were... DEAD!? Some had been transferred or retired.

Which meant that mostly UNAUTHORISED PERSONS WERE LIVING IN THOSE HOUSES. I thought I had a very strong case.

We went to meet Mr. Kichloo, the Deputy Minister in charge of Estates who was the house allotting authority.

When we made our request, he glowered at us and shouted, "WHAT AM I SUPPOSED TO DO, SEND ALL THOSE FAMILIES TO LIVE ON THE ROADS?"

How can you send someone who has already been transferred, retired, or dead anywhere? I wondered. Mr. Kichloo probably believed that the ghosts of the dead would come and haunt him. Anyways, I kept the thought to myself.

Instead I protested, "But sir I am already on the road."

"Sorry, that is not my problem," retorted the Minister and signalled us to leave.

***

Undeterred, we next tried to meet the Deputy Minister's boss, Mr. Ghulam Shah, the PWD Minister (and son-in-law of Sheikh Abdullah) but he acted *busy*. So, we left our written representation with his private secretary.

NOTHING HAPPENED!!!

A few days later, when we followed up with the private secretary, he told us,

"I had a look at your representation and decided NOT to put that up to our Minister. Our Minister gets angry quickly and your representation appeared to be quite rude! He also has a history of having a *tiff* with many IAS officers."

The private secretary left us with no option than to seek an appointment with the Chief Minister. AGAIN.

The great Sheikh Abdullah called us immediately. Maybe he still had some positive feelings about us from his previous interactions. We told him, as frankly as we could manage, all that had happened including the showdown with the Deputy Minister Estates.

The Chief Minister heard us out patiently. But didn't say a word either in our support or against us. We took his leave not knowing whether anything would happen after all.

Four days passed by and each day seemed so long. *God, is this what I had joined the IAS for?*

On the fifth day, a Jamadar (Senior Peon), wearing a very ornate and colourful dress, walked into my office room and saluted me. I was startled. Who wouldn't?

I looked up, and the Jamadar bowed and gave me an *envelope*. I looked at the envelope. It was from the office of the Deputy Minister Estates.

When I opened the envelope, I found an order inside.

As I read, I felt like letting out a loud YIPEEEEEEE.

Yes, I had actually been allotted 26-B, a "B type" (B-grade or whatever) house in Gandhinagar! I was told later that the CM had called the Deputy Minister and had pulled him up for misbehaving with us.

We thought the problem had been solved. We would finally have a house in Jammu!

***

When we went to take "possession" of the house, we found a fat lock hanging on its main door.

The chowkidar told us that the previous occupant had NOT yet "handed over" (to the Estates Department) the house. When he peeped inside, the house seemed empty. There were no belongings. Nothing! Which meant THERE WAS NO ONE LIVING INSIDE.

This was a strange mystery! We decided to investigate the matter.

We soon found out that the house was allotted to an Inspector from IB (Intelligence Bureau), who had just been transferred out of Jammu. But his superiors at IB had put a lock on the house to "reserve" it for the incoming inspector!

So now we understood the game plan of the Deputy Minister. He had given in to the wishes of the CM to allot us a house. And then sabotaged that by sending us to a place which was not in the "possession" of his department.

Not to accept defeat that easily, we sought an appointment with the senior most officer of the IB in Jammu. That was not too difficult.

When we reached his office in Gandhinagar, a posh part of the town, we learnt that he was Ajit Lal, an IPS (Indian Police Service) Officer from the Himachal cadre. When we met him, he told us he was from Bihar too. And how his family knew both mine and Arun's family so well.

Relieved, we told him about our *stupid* problem. Mr. Lal immediately called someone from his office and directed him to ensure that the *keys* to the house were delivered to us *within two hours*.

Then he turned towards us and wondered aloud as to why the State Government had allotted a house to us, to two IAS officers, that was of the *level* suited more to an IB *Inspector*. He also mentioned that the entire government colony in Gandhinagar reminded him of the Gardani Bagh colony in Patna where only clerks used to stay.

We were stunned at the analogy. But as we dug deeper, we knew how right he was.

The Gandhinagar government colony was indeed constructed as *temporary quarters* for the Kashmiri employees coming for the winters to Jammu. Presuming that the investment could be a waste if Kashmir ever joined Pakistan or Jammu became another state, the Kashmir-centric government of the day had spent as little as *Rupees 8000* only on constructing those quarters!

The house was in the pits but beggars couldn't be choosers. We acquired a small fridge and now could preserve our milk, fruit and meals. We also had a house warming party inviting all our colleagues and friends. I cooked single-handedly and Arun did the dishes as we had till then no help.

***

We had no gas connection and so were cooking on kerosene stoves. When Arun's father got to know of that, he told us about the gas connection that Arun had applied for in Gorakhpur some five years back. That had "matured" which was fantastic, as gas connections in those days, like most consumer goods like cars, scooters or watches, were rationed and extremely difficult to come by.

Arun's father volunteered to get a gas cylinder from Gorakhpur, where he was then posted in the Railways, and carried it personally for us in Jammu. It was probably *illegal* to carry a filled gas cylinder in the train but we were so grateful for that kind gesture.

In due course, we got that connection transferred to J&K and thus escaped our dependence on the foul-smelling kerosene stoves.

Having a house reduced my misery nonetheless. And the optimist I am, I again started believing that maybe with my positive attitude I *would* and *could* make a difference.

Little did I know then that our battles with the "Outsiders' Curse" had just begun.

Chapter 5

Fighting for Senior Scale

EVERYWHERE ELSE in the country, IAS officers used to be, quite in routine, promoted to their senior scale of pay after four years of service. Which meant a significant raise in your salary. But as we noticed, getting the senior scale was a big *deal* in J&K. Officers would get it only after five-six years of service and some didn't get it till even in their ninth year!

I remember telling colleagues in the IAS Academy in Mussourie how some of our seniors in J&K were getting sub-divisions after sub-divisions even in their sixth year of service. And the knowledgeable among those were aghast. What? They would blink.

"But when do they get their senior scale then?"

Good question, and now we had to look for the answers.

Facing the dreaded "Departmentals"

WE SOON FOUND out that Mr. Noor Mohammed, the virulently anti-IAS (and anti-everything Indian!) Chief Secretary, had found a superb handle to beat IAS officers with. And that was that they had to *clear* their departmental examinations to be eligible to their first promotion.

Fair enough, we thought. Passing another examination shouldn't be that big a problem for any IAS officer who had beaten almost 300,000 graduates to enter the service.

The problem in J&K was that the departmental examinations were being conducted by the JK Public Service Commission (PSC), and that too NOT every year. Rules were further *rigged* to ensure that IAS officers *didn't* clear these tests in one go.

For example, it was stipulated that unlike other states where IAS officers had to clear tests in only the official language of the state, in J&K the "outsiders" were mandated to pass a test in written Urdu and face an interview to test their knowledge of spoken Kashmiri and Dogri. And there were NO prescribed text books for any of these three languages.

The local IAS officers were exempt from the language tests regardless of whether they knew any of these three languages or not.

The second stipulation was that IAS officers had to get more than *55%* marks to pass when the usual pass percentage anywhere else was between 30-40%.

Beggars couldn't be choosers. We decided that we must clear our departmentals as soon as possible. So, we called on the Chairman PSC and requested him to schedule a test soon.

We studied hard and were able to clear all our papers in one go. Except the language paper where I got stuck for a very interesting reason. My Dogri interviewer was Mr. Teja Singh, a Sikh gentleman from Jammu, who had retired some time back as Director of Hospitality and Protocol, my "favourite" department.

While in service he used to be quite a *butt* of jokes. The most hilarious was when someone looking for a Directory asked him, he thought he meant his wife and said,

"But my Directory (wife) is at home." *Director ki biwi Directory!*

Anyway, in the interview, this gentleman asked me to tell him the story of the "Lady and the Lamb..uh" in Dogri. I was taken aback as I had never heard of such a story even in English. I asked him whether he meant the "Lady and the

Lamp" so that I could talk of Florence Nightingale.

He repeated, "No, Lady and the Lambuh." I had been taught the nursery rhyme of Mary who had a little lamb but here I was being asked for a story. I gave up and told him,

"Sir, I am sorry I don't know about any such story in English or in Hindi and so translating it into Dogri is not possible."

That upset him. So, he asked me what a baby goat is called in Dogri. Now I had memorised so many Dogri words but I didn't know that it was called *"Chhillo."* To cut a long story short, I was failed.

Of course, I didn't give up and continued with my studies and the official assignments. One day, I was surprised to see the same Mr. Teja Singh land up in my lowly office of a Deputy Secretary. He had come to ask me for a favour for his brother who was a government servant and who was being *suspended* for corruption.

I was reluctant. *So, he openly dangled the carrot of passing me in Dogri if I helped him.* I thanked him, but said a firm NO. I also went by the rules and didn't do his *illegal work.*

Fortunately, by the time the next departmental examination dates were announced Mr. Teja Singh had retired. His successor in the PSC was much nicer. So, I managed to pass my language tests with no further hiccups.

We immediately applied for the release of our senior scale, without waiting to complete four years in service. Mr. Noor Mohammad disposed off our "audacious demand" by ruling that we could get it only when we completed *four years* in service.

Death of an Era

LIFE CONTINUED and then came the fateful September of 1982. We were in Lal Chowk in Srinagar shopping for some daily necessities, when suddenly we heard the shopkeepers closing down their shops. The shutters started coming down with a deafening thud. The sound echoed and seemed like an explosion. As if something sinister was about to happen.

"What's the matter?" I asked a shopkeeper.

The shopkeeper looked at me. Fear and terror in his eyes. "Go home. Beta, go home... go home *fast*."

"What's happening?"

"There is a rumour that Sheikh Abdullah is dead," he almost whispered.

"And if that be so, the crowds will soon start beating everyone who looks like 'Indians.'"

"But what have I or any other Indian done?" I was bewildered.

"Listen. Just go back home. Go!" He was now shouting.

The shopkeeper succeeded in scaring us. A mild panic attack set in.

We rushed in our scooter to our flat, now in Tulsi Bagh close to the Bakshi Stadium. Our neighbour was Anil Kumar, who was posted as the Secretary to the Governor. He too had just come home. We asked him and he confirmed that indeed Sheikh Abdullah was *no more*. But for reasons of "law & order," the news had to be kept a secret.

The entire episode was an interesting realisation. Which was that in Kashmir when passions are aroused, NO logic works. Kashmiris are forever the *victims* and their anger must be vented out on someone other than themselves. So, any *Indian (outsider)* would do very well, thank you.

The death of the Sheikh was announced only after his son Farooq Abdullah had reached Srinagar and assumed the charge of the Chief Minister. There was a huge funeral procession the next day. Without caring for our safety, we too joined in. Moving in a sea of humanity, with distraught Kashmiri women singing funeral songs, we reached Sheikh's residence to bid him the final good bye.

***

In the bureaucratic history of J&K, a new phase had begun. Sheikh Abdullah, despite all his personal charisma and good intentions, had got surrounded by sycophants, especially during his last days in office. In the higher echelons of government, this coterie was addressed as the "syndicate." It comprised the Chief Secretary, the Director General of Police, the Secretaries of Planning, Finance, and Forests, and a few others.

To take forward their own *corrupt anti-national agenda,* they would all connive and mislead the CM into doing things which he initially felt were wrong. For example, if the CM knew officer "X" was corrupt and incompetent and yet the syndicate wanted him to be given an important assignment they would all gang up and act in unison.

On a tour, the DGP may set the ball rolling with a casual remark that "X" was a really good officer. The CM would brush aside the comment.

In a meeting with the Forest Secretary next this would be reiterated. By the time all the syndicate had thus whispered in to the CM's ears their good words about Mr. X, the Chief Secretary would take the proposal to give X a "lucrative" assignment and a tired CM would just sign on the dotted line!

Farooq Abdullah on taking over as CM addressed a huge public meeting in Lal Chowk and announced in his trademark flamboyant manner that he would soon hang all corrupt *officers* from the lamp posts of Lal Chowk. Soon thereafter, in the first reshuffle of the bureaucracy, he brought in IAS Direct Recruits to man all senior posts. Noor Mohammed, however, remained the Chief Secretary as with a seniority of 1956 and a half years he was technically the senior most.

We jumped around with joy. It looked like a new era was being ushered into J&K. We could all now hope for a better tomorrow where we would work with all sincerity and dedication and make J&K the crowning glory of India. But was it to be so?

My First Encounter with Bribery

WITH THE CHANGE of government, I also got a change of posting to the Public Works Department (PWD). That was a relief as unlike the Agriculture Department, where we were seven officers in a room, I now had a small but exclusive office room to function from. Although we were still not given a field posting, I at least had *some work* to do now.

However, probably because the department was considered "too lucrative," it was soon split into two, with the Public Health Engineering (PHE) and the Irrigation wings going to Mr N R Gupta, a 1971 batch officer, and Roads and Building (R&B) wing allotted to Mr. H H Tyabji, a 1965 batch officer. Funnily, I a mere Deputy Secretary was reporting to both! Thankfully both were Direct Recruits and "outsiders" and both treated me well. For the first time, I felt valued and was happy working in J&K.

Word soon spread that whatever note I wrote would sail through both secretaries. This resulted in a couple of rather interesting incidents. One concerned Mr. Teja Singh, the redoubtable member PSC, trying to "bribe" me in his own inimitable manner that I have already narrated.

The second was the arrival of Mr. Tiku to my room—the same Mr. Tiku who would serve me with eviction notices at the drop of a hat when we were in the Circuit House Jammu in 1981 during our probation days.

Every year a list of engineers was prepared who were young and healthy enough to be posted to Ladakh, which is a cold and high altitude area. I was in the midst of doing this exercise and learnt that Mr. Tiku's brother an engineer was also figuring in that list. Mr. Tiku wanted me to *remove* his name so *he wouldn't have to bear the hardship of working in Ladakh.*

Very sweetly, I asked him to reconfirm the name of his brother and scribbled it on my notepad. Thereafter I thanked him.

Surprised, Mr. Tiku asked me the reason for being thanked. I reminded him of his behaviour and explained I was thanking him for pointing out the name of his brother in this long list. Otherwise being an "outsider," how could I possibly know who his brother was. Now that I knew, I could ensure that even in Ladakh, which was admittedly an important part of J&K, Mr. Tiku's brother lands up in its remotest corner.

Mr. Tiku's face fell, and he left my room. I am told he next went to the secretary but couldn't get an audience.

Next morning when I woke up I was surprised to find *twenty gardeners* descending on my house. They were trying to spruce up my little garden in Jawahar Nagar, where I had shifted from my government flat in Tulsi Bagh, courtesy my posting in the PWD. Alarmed, I went out to ask what the matter was and learnt that they were deputed by Mr. Tiku who was now the Director of the Parks & Gardens Department. The poor gardeners were instructed to please me. *Alas they failed and Mr. Tiku's brother's posting remained unchanged.*

The third incident concerned an Executive Engineer (XEN) who was posted in Kishtwar, a far-flung region of the then-District Doda, and who wanted to have his posting changed. One day he dropped in to my office, narrated his problem and requested for a transfer to Jammu where he claimed his ailing parents were living, his children were studying, and so on.

The XEN then asked me a direct question—"how much will that be?"

Not being able to understand what he meant, I explained that we were then in the process of making a transfer policy. And that if he has completed his two-year tenure, he could hope to be transferred out soon, and so on. But I could not give him a definite time frame in which the policy would be approved and his transfer orders could follow.

The XEN was getting impatient. So in a monotone, he again repeated his question— "how much will that be?"

I was puzzled and asked him, "what do you mean?"

"How much do I have to pay for that favour?" he clarified.

As I finally "understood" his question, I lost my temper and shouted at him to "Just get out of my room."

Still startled at this first experience of being offered a *bribe*, I rushed to my bosses. Both heard me out patiently and advised me to be "cool" about the incident. Because, as they explained, "nothing in J&K moves without greasing some palms."

Another Deputy Secretary, who belonged to the local Kashmir Administrative Service (KAS), and was almost on the verge of retirement, was much more eloquent. Almost chastising me for my "childish" outburst, he remarked,

"Sonali ji, you've no regard for even Goddess Lakshmi (the goddess of wealth)! Each file here would have a *person* behind it and till *Lakshmi* appears the file should NOT move. You're so stupid clearing files the whole day and going home in the evening leaving only a clean table behind. Mark my words. You will be a terrible *misfit* here."

How true were his words because I remained "stupid" and I remained a "misfit" forever!

Then I came across the pathetic case of an executive engineer who had been placed under *suspension* for over three years. When I examined his file, I found that he had been *wrongly implicated*. Even the vigilance department couldn't establish anything against him and was forced to give him a clean chit. But no one was still processing his case!

When the gentleman first came to my office, he was raving and ranting so much that I thought he had lost his mind. Anyway, I processed his case, and he was soon reinstated in service.

When the orders reached him, he came to my room and before I realised he was bending down to touch my feet in gratitude. This greatly unnerved me. But he said, "Words can't express my gratitude. Because Madam, in J&K, no one ever lifts a little finger to help anyone in trouble unless there are some *considerations* for the same."

The engineer was Mr. C.L. Mattoo, who the country would later know as the unfortunate father of Priyadarshini Mattoo, the girl who was sexually assaulted and murdered by her classmate.

When the Pakoras won

THE MANAGER, Indian Airlines (IA), as I have mentioned, used to be the most important dignitary those days because he controlled the "quotas." He was the only one who could produce an airline ticket which in the absence of any competition from private airlines was a scarce commodity. In the process, he had managed a big ministerial bungalow, next to the residence of the Chief Secretary, which was an eyesore for many.

As Deputy Secretary PWD, I was also looking after Estates. One day Dr. Farooq Abdullah, the Chief Minister called us—the Commissioner Secretary Roads & Buildings, Director Estates and me. With his green blue eyes flashing, Farooq sahib asked us to get the house given to the Indian Airlines Manager *vacated* forthwith.

Being an enthusiastic youngster with the first task given by the Chief Minister himself, I went about it with all the seriousness at my command. We identified another house, of a lower category, and gave a "notice" to the Manager to shift forthwith, or else....

Nothing happened even after the deadline given in the notice expired. While I was contemplating starting eviction proceedings with police help, someone commented that the Indian Airlines Manager has been saying that no one can shift him because the CM loves the *pakoras* (a deep fried savoury) that his wife serves him at his residence in Srinagar.

"What rubbish!" I said.

And went about my task only to be suddenly stopped by an *express direction* from the Chief Minister's office. The *pakoras* had indeed won!

Meeting Mr. Rehman

WHILE I WAS so busy working out such interesting cases in my department, July 1983 had dawned. At last, we had completed *four years* of service.

But NO orders for our promotion to the senior scale had yet been issued although we had *cleared* our departmental exams and had been confirmed in the IAS after completing our training and probation successfully. We had met Mr. Noor Mohammed many times and even sent him innumerable written representations but to no avail.

As I have mentioned, Mr. Noor Mohammed had begun his career as a junior scale stenographer and rapidly rose because of his cunningness and his ability to amass wealth. When the All-India Services were extended to J&K he became a part of its "initial constitution" and was given the seniority of 1956 and a half. He was from a humble background (his father was a Village Chowkidar who in those days had to be paid by the villagers). But when he retired, his assets in Manasbal (near Srinagar now in Ganderbal District) and around were reputed to be worth over Rupees *200 crores (2000 million)*.

Anyway, I realised that with his dislike for all things Indian, except the Indian currency, he was not going to give us our due.

So Arun and I decided to meet Dr. Farooq Abdullah, the Chief Minister. The Principal Secretary to the Chief Minister was Mr. Mehmood-ur-Rehman, a direct recruit officer from Uttar Pradesh, whose run-ins with politicians were legendary. As District Development Commissioner, Ladakh, he was said to have taken on Mr. Ghulam Mohammad Shah, the son-in-law of Sheikh Abdullah and a cabinet minister. Mr. Shah was a hot-tempered person but when he lost his cool in front of Mr. Rehman, the latter retorted equally rudely. But worse was yet to come.

Invoking his inherent magisterial powers, Mr. Rehman disconnected Mr. Shah's phone and confined him to his room in the circuit house till he came to his senses. When a fuming Gul Shah (as he was known) complained to Sheikh Abdullah, Sheikh sahib called both Mr. Rehman and Gul Shah for dinner and tried a patch-up. I have NEVER heard of any such incident in the annals of IAS in India *where in a fight with a minister the officer came out the winner.*

Anyway, when we approached Mr. Rehman, he not only ensured that we got to meet the CM but also that we got our senior scale within a few days.

Getting Senior Scale

OUR JOY WAS unbounded. In J&K, our promotion orders had created history. After years, senior scale had been granted on completion of four years and that too to "outsiders." Our order also included the name of Parvez Dewan who was two years our senior but was being given senior scale with us. However, we had drilled *four years* so much into the head of Noor Mohammad, the Chief Secretary, that Parvez also got it from the time he completed four years in service with arrears.

To firmly establish the four-year rule, I then went to all my seniors and requested them to apply for senior scale from the date it was due to them i.e. from the fourth year. Many did but some like Mr. S.S. Kapur (1974) declared that if everyone gets it, he will too and didn't bother to apply.

So those who applied initially, including Mr. N.R. Gupta (1971), who was my Secretary, and eight year my senior, were all given the senior scale with effect from the date they completed their fourth year, after which Mr. Noor Mohammed put his foot down and said no more.

He also refused to promote several seniors like S.S. Sahni (1974 IAS JK) and Samuel Verghese (1976 IAS JK) because they had still not cleared the departmentals.

As for the ever-so-cocky Mr. S.S. Kapur, he never got his senior scale from the time he completed four years in service, even though he retired as the Chief Secretary of J&K!

Chapter 6

Our First Field Posting

ONLY AFTER GETTING the senior scale could we get our first field posting.

I was posted as Project Officer, Drought Prone Area Programme (DPAP) in Udhampur District while Arun was posted as Project Officer, District Rural Development Agency (DRDA), in the same district.

Thanks to Mr. Ashok Jaitly (IAS 1964 JK), who was the Planning Commissioner, we became the first direct recruit IAS officers to get such "prized" rural development assignments in J&K. To be fair, the Government of India had been insisting in its "guidelines" that IAS officers handle such projects where the outlays were to the tune of millions of Rupees, but who listens to Government of India in J&K?

Looking for a house (and office) for the Kumars

ON LANDING IN Udhampur, the first problem we encountered was, *of course*, of where to stay. Our predecessors were local, Block Development Officer (BDO) rank officials, who had happily stayed in either their own houses or in private accommodations rented from their relatives. Officially too, in the district, there was specifically earmarked accommodation only for the Deputy Commissioner (DC), Superintendent of

Police (SP), District Forest Officer (DFO) and some members of the Engineering Services.

So first we landed up in the private accommodation rented by Arun's predecessor. The building was ill-designed with open drains from the bathroom and kitchen going through the building! What an ungainly sight it was.

The place constantly smelt of rotting flesh. Because as we discovered, the landlord was in the business of buying skins of dead animals and processing them as leather. The place, from an olfactory point of view, therefore, was a living hell.

Using all my goodwill earned in my previous posting in the PWD, and with great difficulty, I could finally get an official house which was previously occupied by an Assistant Engineer of the PWD. The house was well-located, next to the DC's and SP's house and in front of the District Dak Bungalow. It had two bedrooms all right but only one bathroom in-between. In addition, it had a small drawing room, dining area and kitchen.

The kitchen was full of cockroaches. But when we bought an insecticide and asked our office help (yes, for the first time in our lives we had one in Udhampur), "to do the needful," he refused point blank. His logic: cockroaches represented wealth, and no way could he be a party to destroy wealth!

So, tying hankies on our faces we sprayed the "wealth-destroying" insecticide room-by-room ourselves!

The office too was in shambles. And as a lady the biggest problem I faced was—no toilet anywhere in the complex. Anyway, again we looked around and managed to locate a fairly decent space on the third floor of a newly constructed building in the city centre.

The DC, the chairman of both our organisations, was a local promoted IAS officer. He was so thrilled to have two direct recruit IAS officers under him that he supported us fully in our quest to move to "swankier surroundings," as some journalists later commented.

The Drought-Prone Area Development Work

WORK-WISE, MY job was to implement Government of India's "area development" schemes that could help the drought-prone areas of the district improve their yield and living standards. This meant improving the irrigation infrastructure, increasing the forest cover, introducing drought-resistant agricultural practices and so on.

Arun's task, on the other hand, was "beneficiary-oriented." So, while I focussed on area development of the drought-prone areas of the district, Arun had to first get a list of all below-the-poverty level people of the district which he did and put out in the public domain. Then he had to rope in all banks, some 52 of them, to give "income-generating" loans to such poor people. These could be in the shape of milch animals like cows and buffaloes, or load carrying ones like horses, mules and donkeys, or small village level industries of pickle making, etc. Typically, banks provided 50% of the "project cost" and the rest came through Government of India subsidies and the beneficiaries' "margin money."

At the conceptual level, both programmes were great. But what was killing them was the *corruption*, which was rampant at all levels. *Nothing moved without greasing a few palms.* Same set of animals were being rotated from beneficiary to beneficiary for milking the Government of India subsidy.

Both of us, therefore, had to tour intensively, meeting beneficiaries and putting the fear of God in government functionaries. Arun introduced the idea of a weekly animal mandi (marketplace) in Udhampur, next to a pond near the Rural Development office, where buyers, sellers and bank managers could meet each other and conduct business in a transparent manner. The concept proved to be such a runaway hit that the mandi continues to function even today!

As my programme dealt with other government functionaries, I had an additional problem. And that was—that my office had become a conduit for the release of Government of India funds to various departments like Irrigation, Forest, Agriculture, Animal and Sheep Husbandry. Without bothering whether that helped fight drought conditions in the district or not. To my utter horror, this also included paying the salary of some staff in all these "line departments" which was totally prohibited under the guidelines. There were murmurs that the practice suited everyone from top to bottom as they were all taking "cuts" in the process.

With the foolish enthusiasm of a green horn, and with all the knowledge I had gained in my previous assignment as a Deputy Secretary in Agriculture, I plunged headlong in setting things right. First, I drew up a plan of action for the entire district and for all the departments concerned.

The first road block I hit was with the Director Rural Development who was unhappy that his *cut* had been affected. The second was surprisingly the State Planning Department.

For every Government of India scheme, they had to provide for a "matching" state share. This meant that if Government of India was providing Rupees 100, state also had to provide Rupees 100. Since J&K was *perpetually bankrupt*, the only way the Planning Department could do this "matching exercise" was by mentioning the cash value of the staff lent for that programme against its share. Interestingly, they would show this value of the same set of staff against different Government of India programmes hoping that the various ministries in Delhi never catch on!

The Finance Department was doing something even funnier. They would hold on to all Government of India money coming to them, and even use it up as some kind of "ways and means advance" in some other unrelated sector. The result was that very little funds were sent to us in the field for actual development works.

On scrutiny of the guidelines, I found that we could very well have our *own bank accounts* in the name of my office, which was technically a Society registered with the State Government. Then Government of India could send funds directly to us, and could also hold us accountable for the needed results.

So, I got the approval of the DC and opened the bank accounts. Government of India too was happy that at least in some corner of J&K things were moving in the right direction. I also demanded the state share to be sent to the same account which ruffled quite a few feathers. There were murmurs that being an "outsider" *I seemed to have no concern for the local sentiments, sensibilities and aspirations!*

I have repeatedly heard these phrases all my life and ignored it. So, in Udhampur too, I went ahead and developed the first watershed development plan in J&K. The greatest opposition to this was from an obnoxious DFO called Salaria. He was used to taking money under DPAP and using it for buying tonnes of fencing material which, of course, was purchased mostly *on paper*. For him, forest development meant NOT planting of trees but purchase of expensive chain link fencing material. Only!

Salaria was nowhere near being promoted to the Indian Forest Service—the first service devastated in J&K to steal the forest wealth—but was still holding a district level cadre post. In fact, he was so abrasive that in a meeting he told me in front of the DC that while I was objecting to the purchase of material for fencing forest land, I was okay with splurging on a new office in the name of a toilet!!

Surprisingly, such attempts at besmirching my reputation had no impact on the local population who were thrilled to find their work getting done without fear or favour. Being an *outsider* with no personal agenda was a novelty they took some time getting used to.

The Member Legislative Assembly (MLA) of a far-flung area called Gool-Gulabgarh used to praise the Executive Engineer Irrigation no end, in meetings. *That rang a bell* and so I decided to go and see the work myself. There was no road connectivity and so after a point beyond Gool, and till Mahore, I had to trudge *on foot*. Wherever any fast-flowing stream was to be crossed, I had to get on a horseback.

Suddenly on the opposite hillock, I saw what looked like the remnants of an old fort. On enquiry, I learnt it was a hundred feet long concrete structure that was part of an irrigation canal that MY programme was funding. The head or the tail of the canal was yet to be designed. But the contractor (connected to the local MLA) had still gone ahead and made the middle portion.

"But how will water ever flow in this?" I asked incredulously.

My guides shook their heads in disbelief. I realised only an "outsider" could ask such a *stupid question*. The engineer and the MLA had got their *cuts*, so where was the need for water going anywhere for drought alleviation?

I was furious. After returning to my headquarters, I sent a detailed tour note to the Planning Commissioner. Mr. Ashok Jaitly was extremely supportive and rewarded me with a letter of appreciation. He even put in a good word for me to the Chief Minister "for being so foolish" as to venture into an inhospitable territory where no officer would generally go.

A Palace Coup in Srinagar

THINGS, HOWEVER, changed suddenly in Srinagar. There was a "palace coup" and the Chief Minister Dr. Farooq Abdullah was replaced by his brother-in-law Mr. Ghulam Mohammad Shah who was heading a breakaway group of MLAs, each of whom was made a minister. We learnt that this was done at the instance of Mrs. Indira Gandhi, the then-Prime Minister of India, who for some reason was extremely annoyed with the somewhat flamboyant functioning of Dr. Farooq Abdullah.

With the regime change at the state-level, changes followed in the field too. The DC Udhampur Mr. Naseem was changed and an officer of the 1978 batch was posted in his place. This created a piquant situation as this officer was just a year senior to us. We were not even calling him "Sir" but now he was our direct boss. I suppose being a son of the soil and having a rich father-in-law being firmly in the camp of the new Chief Minister was the only thing that mattered.

I remember a function in the local State Guest House called Tara Niwas (the erstwhile residence of Tara Devi, the queen) held in the honour of both the CM Mr. Shah and the Deputy CM Mr. D.D. Thakur. Both Arun and I were standing awkwardly in attendance and were totally ignored while there was a lot of hugging and back slapping for the new DC. The feeling of being an *alien* was now complete.

Our agony in Udhampur was, however, short-lived as soon I had to proceed on maternity leave.

On return, I was posted back in the Secretariat as Additional Secretary Planning. It was a lack lustre post because the element of vision or planning was totally missing in the department. All that one was *expected* to do was to total up all kinds of figures and projections, go to Government of India, make all kinds of stories and tall claims and get funds by hook or by crook!!

Arun was sent back to the Power Development Department but to a non-existent section dealing with non-conventional energy sources. He was not even given a personal assistant.

Yet the self-driven person he is, he went on to frame and register a new state-level agency to deal with new and renewable sources of energy. He named it as the J&K Energy Development Agency (JAKEDA) and became its first CEO.

Chapter 7

Working with Mr. Jagmohan

FORTUNATELY, THE CHAOTIC, unscrupulous, and unethical government under Mr. G.M. Shah did not last long and around February-March 1986 Governor's Rule came to be imposed in J&K.

Interestingly, in other states, the constitution calls for the imposition of "President's Rule" through the Governor of that state. But in J&K, because of the special provisions under the J&K Constitution, it is called "Governor's Rule" although it is imposed only with the prior approval of the President of India!

The distinction, which in practice amounted to nothing, was important to assuage the "pro-freedom" sentiments that the special status of J&K encouraged by design.

The Governor was Mr. Jagmohan, a noted civil servant. From his days in Delhi first as the Vice Chairman of the Delhi Development Authority (DDA) and later as the Lt. Governor of Delhi, we knew he was quite a dynamo of an administrator. His assuming the reigns of governance in J&K upset apple carts everywhere.

The Youngest MD of "Arts Emporium"

MY POSTING WAS one of the first to be changed when I was made the Managing Director (MD) of the J&K Handicrafts, Sales and Exports Corporation with additional charge of the office of Director Handicrafts. Apparently, the Governor was looking for a lady IAS officer with some aesthetic sense and had zeroed in on me. The Chief Secretary Mr. R.K. Takkar (IAS 1961) thought I had gone over his head to the Governor to wrangle this "prestigious" posting and conveyed his disapproval to me openly. My protests that I didn't know Mr. Jagmohan from Adam were of no avail.

Never in the history of this department and corporation was an *outsider* IAS officer allowed to step inside that beautiful heritage building on the banks of river Jhelum that once housed the British Resident in Kashmir. For me too, this was my first full-fledged foray into the heart of Kashmir. As MD, I was dealing with staff that was 95% and artisans who were 100%—Kashmiri.

Jagmohan had similarly asked for a young IAS officer, with some writing flair, to hold the post of Director Information and Public Relations. Strangely, the Chief Secretary suggested Arun's name. So once again, Arun created history by becoming the youngest (and the first direct recruit) IAS officer to hold this "sensitive" post.

It was March, and the secretariat was still in Jammu. But since I was headquartered in Srinagar, I had to leave Arun in Jammu and shift to Kashmir immediately with my one-and-a-half-year-old son in tow. Once again, there was no accommodation, and I had to stay in the Circuit House for quite some time till a house in Tulsi Bagh could be allotted to us. Nonetheless, I was thrilled to be the first direct recruit, first lady officer, first *outsider* and the youngest ever MD to have been posted to the Arts Emporium, as it was then called.

When I dressed in a sari and sporting a *bindi* arrived to take charge, the Manager took me as an *Indian tourist* and very solicitously asked me if he could *help* with whatever I wanted to buy. The look of surprise on his face when I told him I'd come to take over as MD was, as that famous credit card advertisement said, "priceless."

My office, of which one part was the showroom, was located in a beautiful heritage building that as I have mentioned housed the British Residency during Maharaja's days. That's why the road leading to it is still called the Residency Road.

The office was exquisite in all senses of the term. The office table was an ornate fully carved piece of walnut wood. The floor had a wall to wall pure silk Kashmiri carpet. The curtains had crewel embroidery all over. Even the pen stand was made of papier mâché with gold paintwork.

It was like walking into a dream palace. But behind all that opulence and class, was lurking the harsh and ugly reality of an evil corporation. The previous MD was one Mr. Mukhtar Kanth who did NOT belong to any service and was given the post simply because he was related to the-then CM Mr. G.M. Shah. He was quite like a *bull in the china shop* who had created havoc to employee morale by *suspending* as many as 59 employees. In fact, the day I joined, they had all gathered to beat up the-then MD.

Strangely, despite this mismanagement, the State Government of the day was busy projecting the "plight of Kashmiri artisans" to Government of India in a manner that the latter was persuaded to grant Rupees four crores (forty million) to the corporation. This was quite a *manna* from the heavens for Mr. Kanth who then went on to fill up all our showrooms with absolute junk. And I suppose filled up his own (and his masters') coffers well in the process.

The first job for me was to go through those 59 cases of suspended employees. I took these up on priority and was happy to *reinstate* each one of them. *There was absolutely no case against any, except that the-then MD thought they were aligned to the wrong political party!*

In general, the morale of the employees was low because no one was given a posting as per his/her ability, acumen or experience. We had 29 showrooms throughout the country and hence a lot of discretion could be exercised in who could be sent where.

Promotions which were long overdue were not even processed. There was instead a well-entrenched system of pick-and-choose where favouritism ruled the roost. As someone remarked, posting of an "outsider" was like a breath of fresh air from the outside.

Since I knew no one and had no favourites, I could go on posting employees after assessing their abilities. The promotions, which were due, were processed post-haste through internal committees. I started a special "Budget Shoppe" in Srinagar for selling as "seconds" or on as- is-where-is-basis the junk that my predecessor had purchased. The Emporium soon limped back to health.

The support of Mr. Jagmohan in all these endeavours was unbelievable. Though I was a very junior officer, he would maintain direct contact by calling me up once every two-three days. As I gathered, his whole aim was to deliver on *good governance* at breakneck speed in the limited time he had and officers who facilitated this with enthusiasm were his favourites. Again, the *irony* was that the Handicrafts Corporation, which was created by Sheikh Abdullah, to save artisans from the clutches of Kashmiri middlemen, was being rescued and resurrected by Mr. Jagmohan, a *rank outsider*.

Arun as Director PR

MEANWHILE ARUN AS Director Information and Public Relations had almost become Mr. Jagmohan's shadow. His job was to get the Governor a good press, and he succeeded so much that he started incurring the wrath of all political parties. Once while returning to office, which was located on the Residency Road in the heart of Srinagar, Arun noticed an angry mob approaching his official car.

The mob soon turned violent and started throwing stones at Arun's car. The stone hit the car with a massive thud shattering the windscreen. Arun ducked in time but a shard of glass cut his forehead. And he began to bleed.

He got down covering his forehead with a handkerchief which now had a small red spot with his blood. And ran to his office chambers. From a distance, he saw that the mob had surrounded his car and set fire to it. The car was now ablaze with an orange flame. The smell of burning fuel in the air was nauseating.

When I heard the news, I felt giddy. I thanked God that Arun was safe. And that he had sustained no serious injury.

But he had lost his car. That was a calamity. As it took some time getting a new official vehicle. But we were relieved that the arsonists didn't enter Arun's office to assault him. That would have been quite easy as in those days none of us moved around with PSOs (Personal Security Officers) or armed escort vehicles.

Arun suspected anti-national elements in his office behind this incident and shared his misgivings with the Governor. In those days, the Urdu newspapers were not type-set but written out by hand in Persian script. And guess who were the "katibs" (who write out Urdu in long hand) doing "kitabat" for all the Urdu newspapers in Srinagar? Government employees of the Information department! This fact was known to everyone. But now was added the element of assault and active sabotage that could no longer be tolerated.

Mr. Jagmohan was swift in his action. First, he closed down all Information department offices outside the state in places like Delhi, Bombay, Calcutta, Jallandhar, etc. Next, he ordered that Arun doesn't route his files through the Secretary Information but through the Chief Secretary. Never in the history of Indian bureaucracy such an action was taken in which a Director was ordered to bypass his own Secretary officially!

The Governor also approved Arun's proposal to have an official advertisement policy so as to eliminate such rags which were printed only when a government advertisement was issued to them. He even allowed Arun to operate a secret fund, like intelligence agencies, with no questions asked.

Meanwhile, there was disturbing news trickling in from all parts of the valley: of Kashmiri Pandits being attacked and their temples being burnt down. Mind you, this was still 1986, but it gave an ominous indication of things to come. We were told that Mr. Mufti Mohammed Sayeed, who later became the Home Minister of India, was *allegedly* behind all these activities to discredit Governor's rule.

A sad outcome of all this was that the original Residency building I sat in was burnt down by terrorists in the 1990s. It was re-built with the generous help from the Government of India much later.

Learning from Mr. Jagmohan

WE LEARNT A lot from Mr. Jagmohan's style of functioning. He sure had his priorities clearly etched out but what was more remarkable was the way he used to follow up on his directions. We saw him carrying a reddish diary in which he would write the instructions he gave to each and every officer. These he used to then review every Saturday and woe betide you if you didn't have a good explanation for your tardiness.

Laggards were ruthlessly cast aside as the Governor couldn't be bothered with their lineage or political connections. Every legendary IAS or IPS officer of the cadre was dumped by him rather unceremoniously. This included even Mr. R.K. Takkar (1961 IAS JK), the Chief Secretary.

Some 14 senior most officers from other departments were just dismissed from government service. This included the Chief Engineer father of two brothers, of which one brother is currently a prominent National Conference leader and the other a Minister of State in the Government of India. Unfortunately, after the end of Governor's Rule, all these corrupt and anti-national officers re-joined the government on court interventions.

Being an extremely hard-working person, Jagmohan would work almost 16 hours a day. He would have a morning-evening walk all-right but would NOT play golf that most other Governors were so fond of. This was quite a change as the heads of government I had seen so far had all a lackadaisical attitude towards issues of governance.

Jagmohan was one person who felt strongly that certain institutional reforms were required to put J&K back on the rails. Admissions to engineering and medical colleges in those days were done in the secretariat and only children of the *rich*, or of *powerful politicians* and *bureaucrats*, could get such coveted seats. This he abolished in one stroke by creating BOPEE or the Board of Professional Entrance Examinations. Similarly, he created the SSRB or the Sub-Ordinate Services Recruitment Board to ensure both transparency and fairness in the recruitment in subordinate services.

In another bold move, Mr. Jagmohan took away all the discretionary appellate powers of Ministers and gave it to a unique institution called the "Special Tribunal." This Tribunal exists even today and both I and Arun had the privilege of functioning as its chairperson later.

Similarly, he set up a full-fledged Institute of Management and Public Administration (IMPA) for continuous in-service training of IAS, KAS and other state officers.

The boldest step was the taking over of the Shri Mata Vaishno Devi Shrine in some kind of a mid-night coup and its management by an autonomous Shrine Board which is today a model for managing religious bodies throughout India.

Mr. Jagmohan also went out of the way to promote local officers into the IAS. The parallel cadre which Mr. Noor Mohammed had created so assiduously over the years was laid to rest. At least temporarily.

No one including bureaucrats of the rank of Chief Secretary were paying income tax in the valley. There was no TDS (tax deduction at source) and what civil servants were doing was to pay no tax for 11 months and then for the 12th month, delay drawing the salary till income-tax officers stopped monitoring the treasuries that disbursed salaries.

Shopkeepers and businessmen, of course, were just not used to paying any income tax. Mr. Jagmohan put the fear of God in them by getting a special team of Income Tax officers from Delhi to raid them. Local officers of unimpeachable integrity were roped in to escort the team and even Arun was drafted to accompany a team to raid a shop in the Hari Singh High Street area. The operation was such a secret that neither I, nor Arun, nor any of Arun's bosses had any clue where Arun was to be the whole day!

While the general public was going ga-ga over such revolutionary developments, there was sullenness in some bureaucrats who felt side-lined. One was my boss, the Commissioner/Secretary Industries and Commerce, Mr. H.H. Tyabji (1965 IAS JK) who hated it whenever Mr. Jagmohan spoke directly to me on telephone even when I was in a meeting with Mr. Tyabji. Those days we did not have mobiles, and Mr. Jagmohan's instructions were that whenever we left our home or office, we must indicate where we were going. This way he could contact us at any time during the day or night.

Revitalising Kashmir Handicrafts

AMONGST THE VARIOUS activities, we undertook to give Kashmir Handicrafts the pre-eminence it deserved, one needs a special mention. With the generous financial help from the Ministry of Commerce, I organised the first international buyer-sellers meet in Srinagar. Buyers from 12 countries agreed to come. But sellers? That was a problem.

I was clear in my mind that we had to do away with exploitative middle men. This I had been doing for all my purchases for the Emporium. So, I chose genuine craftspeople and let them directly interact face-to-face with international buyers with my Emporium standing as a guarantor and facilitator for completing export formalities. The meet was a grand success. But the poor outsider me, didn't know of the fall out. The middle men who were all members of the various

Chambers of Commerce and Industry in Kashmir were seething.

"How dare this Hindu Indian lady come and shake us up, reach out to craftspeople directly, talk of their welfare, and empower them! She must be taught a lesson!"

A nasty letter was sent to Mr. Jagmohan, levelling all kinds of wild allegations against me, with a copy to me. I took the letter and went up to the Governor. Before I could say anything, he remarked, "I have received the letter and did what it deserved. Threw it into the dustbin. "

I was speechless and went back to work with renewed enthusiasm.

Our beings the "favourites" of Mr. Jagmohan had to have a backlash but I would come to that a little later.

Chapter 8

Shopping with the President's Daughter

MY STINT IN the Handicrafts Corporation in 1986 was full of interesting incidents, but one "protocol duty" incident just stands out.

The President of India had come to Srinagar along with his daughter. They were staying at the beautiful State Guest House in the Dachigam Wildlife Sanctuary, on the outskirts of Srinagar. Nothing unusual about that as Kashmir has always been a favourite holiday destination for the high and mighty in India. Hardly a year would pass when we would not have the President or the Prime Minister (or both) in Kashmir driving the administration crazy.

Earlier while I was in Baramulla, I was put on duty to receive Mrs. Indira Gandhi, the-then Prime Minister, who was visiting some forward Army posts. Despite being just a year old in service, Mrs. Gandhi had then floored me with her charm and kindness.

I was then not wrong in expecting a similar experience when I was put on duty with the President's daughter. First, there was a sightseeing trip to the Mughal Gardens, which went off well thanks to the excellent arrangements made by the State Floriculture and Hospitality & Protocol departments.

The daughter, let us call her Ms. M, was pleased and then expressed a wish to buy silk saris.

Buying 35 Silk Sarees

SO, I TOOK THE lady to the Raj Bagh Silk Factory which is a government undertaking and at that point produced the best silk chiffon saris in Kashmir. Ms. M happily selected as many as *35 saris*, each costing between a thousand to fifteen hundred rupees. I gasped as my salary at that point was about 1500 rupees per month. When it came to payment, Ms M declared imperiously that she was not carrying *her purse*. I looked at the ADC from the Navy who was accompanying her. He searched his various pockets and came out with about five hundred rupees.

The Manager of the factory who was also a government employee looked extremely perturbed. He looked at me, an ostensibly senior IAS officer of J&K cadre, silently imploring me to do something. So, I stepped in and gently told Ms. M that since this was a government show room we couldn't take out anything *without* payment.

"I will get all the saris packed Mam and tomorrow when we move to the airport, we can pick it up after payment," I offered in as polite a tone as I could manage.

Ms. M did not look happy but couldn't do much about it. Little did I know that this was only the light thunder before the proverbial deluge.

Raiding MY Emporium

THE NEXT MORNING the Lady descended upon MY Emporium. By now she had been joined by another sister and her family and they were all over the Arts Emporium lustily selecting Pashmina or Shahtoosh (which was not banned then) shawls, silk carpets, Papier mâché—and what not. *I could feel alarm bells ringing hard in my head.*

So, I called aside the Manager of my showroom and told him to ensure that nothing left the showroom *without* payment. I next walked up to the ADC and asked him whether he had arranged for the *money* today in view of the heavy shopping that was going on. In his smart-alec way, the ADC remarked,

"Mrs. Kumar what will you do if we simply take all the stuff and walk out?"

My reaction was immediate.

"Look Lt. Commander (equivalent of Major in Army), I am the custodian of the artisans of Kashmir. And if you do anything like what you described, I would consider that a *daylight robbery*. I shall then go to the police station, which is just outside my Emporium gates, as you may have noticed and register a case. Also as my husband happens to be the Director Information, I shall invite the press to come and see what the first family of India does when they come to a poor state like J&K."

The ADC looked at me in horror, "You can't be serious!"

"Oh yes, I am and I'm crazy enough to do as I just said."

Seeing the mad glint in my eyes, the ADC walked up to the Lady, and I saw her face turning a tomato red. Some phone calls were made and a local Sikh businessman turned up and paid for all that had been bought.

Ms. M was so angry that she did not speak a word to me thereafter. In fact, she did not allow me to sit with her in her vehicle and escort her any further. So, we went to the airport in separate vehicles. I was convinced that I was bidding my career good bye.

At the airport, the two advisers to the Governor, Mr. Qureshi and Mr. Naresh Chandra were sitting along with the Chief Secretary, Mr. B.K. Goswami. At the earliest opportunity, I narrated the whole incident to them in one breath and was ready to be *reprimanded*. But instead they all burst out laughing.

One of them commented, "How right Mr. Jagmohan was, when he had said that Ms. M is a nuisance wherever she goes.

And had added that the only one who can handle her is Sonali. So why don't we put her on duty with Ms. M?"

Wish I had known!

To use an "outsider" to fix an "outsider"? How clever!

Chapter 9

Banished to Ladakh

MY FABULOUS STINT at the Handicrafts Corporation could not continue for long. Nor could the feverish pace of development in J&K that Mr. Jagmohan had unleashed.

For some strange political reason, Rajiv Gandhi, the-then Prime Minister ignored Mr. Jagmohan's advice that the forthcoming state elections be held under Governor's Rule in a "free and fair" atmosphere. Soon we heard of a Rajiv-Farooq accord being signed with Dr. Farooq Abdullah parachuting straight into the Chief Minister's chair.

It was alleged that Farooq's party, the National Conference, rigged the state elections in 1987 on a massive scale. It is also believed that this rigging led to the emergence of Syed Salahuddin, the dreaded Hizbul Mujaheedin Chief. Yousuf Shah (the real name of Syed Salahuddin) was till then just an ordinary worker of a rival political outfit.

On some flimsy charges, police arrested Yousuf. We learnt that a senior minister of Farooq's cabinet visited him in jail and beat him up mercilessly with his own hands! All such atrocities and denial of genuine democratic opportunities ushered in a new restless phase in Kashmir's history we are now so familiar with.

For us, however, it was time to say "goodbye" to our current assignments. To be frank, we knew what was in store for us. Arun had to be *punished* for getting Jagmohan a good press!

And I for shaking up the well-established middleman mafia operating in the Kashmir Handicrafts sector at "Jagmohan's behest."

Which also meant we could now be posted to different towns. Say, I, to Kupwara in Kashmir and Arun to Poonch in Jammu some 700-kilometres apart!

It was like we were about to be given a death sentence but also the freedom to choose how we were supposed to die. *How will you like to die: by beheading, blown to pieces or thrown off from a cliff?* We chose to be thrown off the cliff. At least there was a slight chance for our survival!

To do that, we immediately sought an audience with Mr. M.U. Rehman (1966 IAS JK) who was Farooq Abdullah's Secretary, once again. Mr. Rehman heard us out and agreed with our apprehensions.

"So, what's your suggestion," he asked us point blank.

"Sir, send one of us as DC Leh and the other as Chief Executive of the Desert Development Agency at Leh. That way you can keep us together and also give out the impression that we have been punished," we had prepared our response carefully.

"Good idea. Let me see what I can do," Mr. Rehman had no hesitation accepting our suggestion. He had himself been a legendary DC of Ladakh and knew that Leh was the only district in J&K that had been accommodating two IAS officers of our seniority for quite some time.

We were relieved because earlier when we had made the same suggestion to Mr. Takkar (1961 IAS JK), who also had been DC Leh, he had dismissed us with the remarks,

"You really think I'd agree to hand over the whole district to a single family?"

Arun had to proceed for a compulsory in-service course at the Administrative Staff College of India (ASCI) Hyderabad and I tagged along, at my expense, with my two-year son in tow. Mr. Naresh Chandra, one of the advisers of Mr. Jagmohan was also on the same course. It was he who showed us a news item in the local edition of the Hindu newspaper the next morning announcing gleefully,

"Jagmohan's favourites posted to Leh."

Mr. Naresh Chandra was a little unhappy at the apparent "injustice" but we were beside ourselves. At least there were no nasty surprises like I being sent to Kupwara in Kashmir and Arun to Poonch in Jammu, as some of our "well-wishers" had threatened.

On the completion of Arun's course in Hyderabad, we went to Srinagar to pack up. Arun talked to Mr. SS Kapur (1974 IAS JK) who was then the DC in Leh about his convenience and November 25, 1986 was agreed as the date for the "handing-over-taking-over" function.

Surprisingly, at both our farewells in Srinagar, many of our subordinates wept openly. My Arts Emporium employees and the craftsmen kept on muttering, "Our golden period is over."

Chaman Lal, One of Arun's PA, and a Kashmiri Pandit cried non-stop. He also kept on blabbering that our son will not survive Ladakh's winter, which was spooky.

The Zozila Pass to Ladakh had closed, trapping many trucks which were returning from Leh. All those drivers and passengers had to be rescued on a war footing.

On the personal front, the road closure meant that all our luggage had to be now transported by air. Most of our belongings could be packed in cartons. But what about Arun's beloved scooter, his "Herbie" that had taken us to so many picnic spots in J&K? And my sole Godrej steel almirah with a mirror that also served as my dressing mirror?

Incidentally, this was the only almirah we had which could be locked. And so, before going to office we would lock up our prized possessions like our Phillips 2-in-1 radio cassette player and our Sumeet small mixer-blender in this, every day.

With a heavy heart, we talked to our neighbours and sold both our possessions, i.e. the scooter and the steel almirah, at rock-bottom rates. With the remainder still coming to about 1000 kg., Indian Airlines took a week to transport them all to Leh, as our "personal baggage."

In the process, we created a dubious world record of sorts in the sense that till then no airlines anywhere in the world would have transported so much of "personal baggage!"

As poor *outsiders*, we had no home or relatives to leave our precious possessions with. The Outsider's Curse was now truly upon us.

Surviving the Cold

THAT YEAR THE winter was more severe than usual. The night temperatures in Leh were reaching -20 degrees C. We had a typical problem. We were *homeless* again.

The outgoing Deputy Commissioner Mr. S.S. Kapur had stocked up for the winters and was quite reluctant to move out. Anyway, he had no choice but to "hand over the charge" but he added a caveat that the DC's Residence would be given to us only after *a month* as his family wanted to stay on in Leh.

What could we do?

We had a small baby, hardly two years old, and the circuit house was most ill-equipped to handle any guests during the winter months. A coal *bukhari* would be lit all right and the room would soon become warm enough to sleep in. But the ambers would die by about 1:30 a.m. and then the freeze would set in—literally. I would regularly see the milk in a cup left over by my son turning to ice by morning.

There was no running water or electricity. My son's nappies washed (I had no access to any disposables in those days) and put out in the sun to dry would instead be frozen stiff by the evening. The water in the flush as well as in the water closet would turn to ice every night. And had to be thawed in the mornings by pouring in some boiling water! It was all a grand mess.

Leh town was also slowly running out of stock. In any

case, things like dals (lentils) were quite unheard of in Leh at that time. Fresh fruits and vegetables also vanished, and we were left with only cabbages, carrots, potatoes and turnips. These vegetables used to be buried about four feet below the ground so that they didn't freeze and remained somewhat edible, provided you could stand the slightly fermented smell!

Anyway, the Kapur family left after about 15 days and we could finally move in. The DC's house was one of the nicest old-style buildings in Leh. The walls of the master bedroom were packed with 56 inches (142 cm) of mud which insulated this house from the cold quite well. It was never below zero degrees inside the house even with no heating. The water closet too never used to freeze in this house.

We had no quilted heavy windcheaters but my office had some in stock. These came in handy till a resourceful Ladakhi charged us 100 GBP (more than our month's salary) to get us an Everest-grade down jacket from the UK.

Arun in one of his earlier assignments as CEO JAKEDA (J&K Energy Development Agency) had got a modern fuel efficient cast-iron coal *bukhari* designed by Dr. Ashok Gadgil, then a scientist at TERI (Tata Energy Research Institute) in Delhi. We were the first beneficiary of this gleaming *bukhari*—gleaming literally because it was painted with silver reflective paint and had shark-style fins all around.

That was quite a conversational piece in any party and actually quite a life saver. Now my coal used to last the entire night and the temperatures inside used to hover around plus 30-degree C when the outside temperatures used to dip below minus 20 degrees.

I used to carry that *bukhari* as a souvenir for quite some time till it got stolen, hopefully by someone who needed it more. There were plans to fabricate these *Bukharis locally* in Ladakh but I think the coal mafia intervened and scuttled the project. A more efficient *bukhari* would have reduced their allocation of coal which they could "ill-afford."

Cold Arid Desert Development

WORK WISE, BEING a cold arid desert, the challenges of development in Ladakh were totally different from any other part of J&K. The barren landscape barely yielded some fodder for the famed pashmina goats. But these goats were bred by nomads above 14,000 feet. What do you do then for the region between 10,000 to 14,000 feet?

After numerous brainstorming sessions with the villagers and experts in the sheep husbandry department, we made a project for introducing Angora goats in this problem area. We argued that this would help the farmers get another quality of wool and cheaper meat (than that obtained from the pashmina goats) and help improve their living standards in due course.

Armed with a detailed project report, I ventured in the labyrinthine *Ministry of the Rural Development, Government of India, Delhi*. This was the Ministry which was funding my Desert Development project in any case. The reaction of the Director in the department in Delhi was amazing. He screamed,

"GOATS—in a *desert area*! No, that can't be permitted. Why don't you make a project for camels instead?"

I was flummoxed, but the Director wasn't being sarcastic. He had only dealt with the issue of desert development in Rajasthan (which in any case is a hot desert) and could not even comprehend the concerns of the cold arid areas of Ladakh.

"But Sir, there are only forty-four Bactrian (double-humped) camels in the Nobra region. They are tourist attraction alright, but increasing their population can't have as much impact on the region's economy as Angora goats can," I tried to argue.

But it cut no ice.

So, I went a level up to the Joint Secretary who repeated what the Director had said. Additional Secretary? Same thing. It was a resounding—NO, NO, NO everywhere.

I came back disappointed.

Meeting Rajiv, Sonia, Rahul and Priyanka Gandhi

A MONTH ELAPSED. It was now December. The days were exceptionally sunny but the day temperatures were still around minus 12-degree C. One morning we got word that the-then Prime Minister (PM) of India Mr. Rajiv Gandhi would be coming for a day to Leh on 12 December 1986.

We couldn't believe the audacity. The water and sewer pipes of the circuit house were already frozen solid for the last two months. Arun as DC had to put in a couple of workers with blow torches to thaw them in case the Prime Minister "got stuck" in Leh for the night!

The 12 December morning was a little overcast. We were all lined up at the airport to receive the PM. Many were silently wishing that his flight didn't land. Leh Airport's approach is so narrow that at the slightest loss of visibility flights used to abort landing. But being a pilot himself, we learnt that the PM sat in the cockpit and guided the Indian Airlines pilots to land the aircraft safely.

PM had come along with a rather large entourage. It included his Secretary Sarla Grewal, Joint Secretary Mr. Wajahat Habibullah (1968 IAS) who was from our cadre, Mr. M.J. Akbar (the then-Editor *Telegraph*) and Mr. Mani Shankar Iyer, who was also a Joint Secretary in the PMO. And then I saw Mrs. Sonia Gandhi alighting with her children Rahul and Priyanka.

My duty was to escort Sonia and her children to the famous Hemis monastery. I suggested that they don something warmer but Sonia had one look at the ungainly *army parkha* we were offering and refused to wear anything over her *smart* Delhi jacket.

We took almost an hour reaching Hemis. It was so bitterly cold that I could see the cheeks of Sonia turning blue. The monks were gracious enough to offer us a hot bowl of Ladakhi salt tea. Tea done, the children asked to see the famous Hemis dance.

We were aghast. Apparently, no one had told the PM's family that the Hemis festival is organised during the summer months. During winters, most monks leave for other warmer monasteries all over India.

Dejected, and chilled to the bone, PM's family returned to Leh post-haste!

Arun was escorting the PM through the small Leh Bazaar. Ladakhis had come out *en masse* to wave at the PM. Suddenly, to the shock of security personnel, Rajiv got down from his vehicle and started walking. He was smiling from ear to ear and waving enthusiastically. He was also walking rather briskly which you don't do at 12,000 ft. altitude without proper acclimatisation.

Arun found the rather fit PM panting and walked up to him to caution.

"Sir, this is a high-altitude area and if you don't mind may I suggest that you walk a little slowly," he whispered.

Rajiv very sportingly took the advice and slowed down. He also took out his 35mm Leica and started shooting.

Suddenly, he looked at his frame counter and remarked, "Hey, I'm running low on film. Can I get a roll here?"

Mind you, he was looking for a film roll on 12 December 1986 when not a single photography shop was open in Leh's bazaar.

But Arun, a keen photographer himself, didn't bat an eyelid and asked, "Slide or print Sir?"

"Slide, if possible," Rajiv was a little surprised.

"What speed Sir?" Arun had one more question.

"200 should be Okay, what do you think?" the PM asked. He was obviously enjoying this little technical side discussion with a fellow photographer.

"200 ASA should be perfect for today's weather, Sir. I'll just organise that," Arun replied.

By then the entourage had reached the circuit house. While the PM was escorted to the VVIP suite, Arun rushed to the DC's residence, which was next door, and took out an Ektachrome 200 ASA slide film roll from his own stock and rushed back to hand it over to the PM.

We wondered if Rajiv ever caught on to the fact that the slide film was NOT bought from any shop. But he was gracious enough to send us a general "Thank You" letter when he reached Delhi. We were so thrilled that we still carry that letter till this day!

I too had by then reached Leh. PM and Sonia were to leave for a public meeting. Wajahat caught hold of me and asked if there was anything the Prime Minister could announce.

I remembered my Angora goat project and with trembling hands handed over a project copy. The idea appealed so much that the PM in the public rally announced the launch of this project with much fanfare. The poor Department of Rural Development in Government of India had to fall in line and *sanction* my project on instructions from the Prime Minister's Office. The Angora goats were finally procured from Texas USA and were a great success in Leh.

Touring in Leh

WITH THE PM'S visit out of the way, we now embarked on a mission to cover every nook and corner of Leh District. The winter was actually a blessing because there was no traffic on the roads. And where there were no roads, our *Jongas*- the SUVs supplied by the army, didn't need any because the earth was frozen stiff. Little snow that fell on the grounds was like sand that could be literally swept away with a broom.

So, we went to *Pangong lake, Nyoma, Chumathang, Tsomoriri* and all other places that we wanted to visit. Our two-year-old son accompanied us everywhere including on the Leh-Manali road where we had to once spend a most uncomfortable night in an alpine tent. Most other places had some kind of a government rest house but without running water or electricity, of course.

I still remember, when we woke up, our breath had formed small crystals of ice all over the roof of the tent!

Our trip beyond *Khardungla* (the highest motorable pass in the world) to Nobra valley was awe-inspiring. We saw real sand dunes (at 11,000 ft.) and the famed double-humped Bactrian camels, finally. Then we wanted to visit Turtuk, the last village of Nobra valley that was "liberated" from Pakistan's clutches only in 1971.

En route, we had to cross Bogdang, a Buddhist village that had a long-standing irrigation water dispute with Turtuk, which was predominantly Muslim. The villagers of Bogdang apprehended that if our entourage went to Turtuk, we would favour the latter. So, they blocked our road and didn't allow us to go ahead.

Arun was so furious that he ordered our cavalcade to return to Diskit, Nobra's headquarters and drove to Thoise to meet the Wing Commander in-charge Air Force. Using DC Leh's special emergency powers, he commandeered a huge MI-17 helicopter and flew straight to Turtuk with all his 15 district heads, including me.

Turtuk villagers were ecstatic. They were dancing, playing trumpets and shouting "Hindustan Zindabad (Long live India)". We discovered that they had no love lost for Pakistan. But they had genuine problems with their land records being left in Skardu, in Pakistan. They also had the usual demands about irrigation, health, education, etc. which we all made note of and promised to redress. We took the MI-17 back to Leh avoiding the treacherous Khardungla.

The Education Mess in Leh

BACK IN LEH, a horrible news awaited us. The class X school results were announced and EVERY student in the district had failed. The reason: most schools had no teachers.

But why were the vacancies not filled up? Because teacher recruitment was such a *scandal* in J&K. Anyone who tried to do a fair job was subjected to vicious political witch-hunts.

The examples were: Mr. SD Singh (IAS 1968 JK) and Mr. Amit Kushari (IAS 1970 JK), who were still answering charge sheets about their attempts to recruit teachers while they were posted as DCs in Poonch.

So, should we too, like our predecessors in Leh, adopt an ostrich like attitude and pretend the problem didn't exist? Obviously not. We were such bull-headed officers after all!

After considerable brainstorming, Arun decided to tackle the challenge headlong. First, he ordered that we advertise the vacancies well for inviting ample applications. Second, he decided to hold recruitment camps at block headquarters so that maximum eligible applicants of that block could attend. And third, he used his earlier Information Department to *tape* all interviews. The last was to help face any enquiry that could be ordered to investigate the *fairness* or otherwise of the entire recruitment exercise.

The effect was extraordinary. Not a single MP, MLA, or VVIP brought any pressure to favour anyone. Of course, the interview process brought out some *horrifying facts* about the general declining standards of education in the district. For example, many applicants for the post of Maths teachers couldn't answer what was greater: ¼ or ½. Many chose ¼!

And what happened to those dozens of cassette tapes that had recorded those interviews? We carried them for the next 20 years or so in the hope that we'd be now investigated. But alas that pleasure was not to be ours!

Introducing Greenhouses

WINTER PRESENTED all kinds of challenges in Ladakh. Fruit trees instead of growing taller used to shrink an inch or two every winter. Eggs could not hatch. Vegetables used to just wilt up and die.

Having faced the shortage of fresh vegetables myself, I was determined to do something about this problem. I spoke to the Department of Non-Conventional Energy, Government of India, and cajoled them to set up five greenhouses, 100% at their cost, for experimenting with vegetable growing, poultry rearing and egg hatching, fruit plant nursery, and fodder growing for sheep and goats—everything that had problems surviving the harsh winters of Ladakh. These were huge (and expensive) structures made with top quality specifications including double-layered automotive grade toughened glass, marine quality plywood, glass wool insulation etc. which no ordinary farmer could afford. But these were good enough for departmental experimentation needed for establishment of "best practices" protocols.

So, on my next trip to Delhi, I and Arun dropped in the office of the IPCL (Indian Petrochemicals Ltd.) a Government of India undertaking and persuaded them to give us a roll of UV stabilised plastic, which was much cheaper than toughened glass. This could be attached to almost every house in Leh to cover their sunnier, south facing wall to enable them to grow something green like spinach in winters. The experiment was a roaring success and today such plastic green houses are ubiquitous in the entire Ladakh region.

But in the government, I was having *tremendous problems* with my fellow bureaucrats. Mr. S.S. Rizvi (IAS 1965 JK) was the Planning Commissioner and having been posted as DC in Leh earlier considered himself quite an *expert* on Ladakh. He was *furious* at the introduction of such *alien* concepts as *Angora goats* or *greenhouses*.

"Have you read Moorcroft and Cunningham? Did they ever suggest greenhouses? Are you going to change the way Ladakhis eat by introducing tomatoes and greens in their diet," he confronted me one day.

"But Sir, Ladakhis are already eating rice (from government ration shops) and Amul Butter. In fact, we have persuaded the Leh Cooperative to get some frozen meat too, from companies like Al-Kabeer, which has also been quite a hit," I replied cheekily.

Mr. Rizvi wasn't convinced!

Then I picked up courage to tell Mr. Rizvi that of the two British gentlemen he had named, one had come to buy horses and the other to see how the British Empire could be expanded to reach Tibet. And yes, I had read both and found them pretty irrelevant to the task I was in-charge of.

It was only much later that I realised the consequences such an "attitude" could have on my ACRs (Annual Confidential Reports) which is what governs an IAS officer's entire career.

Getting in to the Cross-Hairs of "Locals"

A MUCH BIGGER bone of contention was my idea of introducing sprinklers and going in for drip irrigation. I firmly believed that this would help improve productivity and could optimally utilise the available, rather meagre, water resources of Ladakh. I spoke to the Irrigation Engineer concerned and ordered that tenders be floated. However, I soon realised that the engineer himself had no idea what I was talking about and, therefore, considered it prudent to abandon the whole idea. The tenders in any case had elicited a very tepid response.

Meanwhile the people, whose vested interests I had hurt, had complained to my superiors. Soon I found a *written explanation* called from me by Sushma Chaudhary, the state Agricultural Secretary, to explain how I could even think of such an *atrocious* idea as using drip or sprinkler irrigation in Ladakh. Mind you, I had NOT wasted any government money on procuring any item till then. But had only invited bids and abandoned the idea.

The entire episode left a bitter taste in the mouth. I realised that it was not only the politicians but our own colleagues who were such impediments to change. They seriously believed that things should go on as they had always been without ruffling any feathers. If you do anything new, anything different, you are shaking up the system.

And the empire will then strike back.

Sushma Choudhary was holding another stupid grouse against me—that I hadn't bothered to receive her at Khaltsi, the border of Leh District, when she was coming for a state cabinet meeting at Leh. No protocol warranted that! But all other district level officers of the Agriculture Department had gone to receive her at Khaltsi. So, I was immediately put on the "hit list."

That earlier I had gone to her in Srinagar and personally invited her to stay with me in Leh cut no ice. I had pleaded with her that the Leh Circuit House had just two decent rooms which will have to go to CM and a senior cabinet minister. So, if she insisted on NOT staying with me, she was bound to get the worst room in the circuit house. And this was exactly what happened.

The Chief Secretary Mr. Khosla (IAS 1962 JK) knew what he was in for. So, after Sushmaji's refusal, when we invited Mr. Khosla to stay with us in the DC's guest room, that had an independent entrance, he happily accepted.

Later when Ms. Sushma Choudhary and other senior officers like Sheikh Ghulam Rasool tried to spoil our Annual Confidential Reports (ACRs), it was he who stepped in to expunge entries from Arun's report. Unfortunately, my report didn't go through him. So, I was saddled with a nasty ACR that in tune with the prevailing norms of those times was NEVER communicated to me. That meant that I had NO opportunity to offer any defence.

The first thing the coterie did to harass us was in the District Development Board meeting in Leh. This was a practice started by Sheikh Abdullah in which the entire cabinet led by the Chief Minister would visit every district of the state once a year to review matters and take decisions on-the-spot. In Leh, no one raised the matter of school teacher recruitment BUT THEY

UPBRAIDED ARUN FOR THE ZERO PASS PERCENTAGE OF LEH STUDENTS!

The Revenue Minister asked Arun to explain his disposal of Agrarian Reforms cases when Leh had hardly any tenant-landlord kind of disputes. Why, Ladakh hardly had any land disputes too because under an order of the Maharaja, a Ladakhi could own any amount of land that he could fence, irrigate and cultivate.

Someone asked us if we had done any touring and refused to believe when we pointed out the number of places we had spent nights in. The maximum number of nasty, sarcastic and negative comments were passed by Sheikh Ghulam Rasool and Ms. Sushma Choudhary.

Something was brewing. And the opportunity soon presented itself in the form of the visit of the President of India.

Because "I don't sleep with the President"

IT WAS SEPTEMBER 1987. The President of India landed up with his wife and two grand-children. Being the Supreme Commander of the Armed Forces, and considering the vast resources that the army had in Leh, we hoped his entourage would stay with the army. But the President, probably to make himself more accessible to the local politicians, declared that he would stay with the civil administration.

So, the VIP room in the circuit house was spruced up. The room next to the VIP room was readied for the grand-children. The third room went to Mr. R.S. Chib, the Cabinet Minister who had to escort the President.

The President on arrival went for a meeting with the army where the army very stupidly asked the accompanying Minister to keep away. They had kept a chair for Arun but how could Arun let the Minister stew outside and occupy a seat inside? Mr. Chib being an ex-Air Force officer took the slight very seriously and upbraided poor Arun for mismanaging the (army) function!

Meanwhile I accompanied the lady President to the circuit house. I took her first to the VIP room, which she gave a glance over, cursorily. She then demanded to see *her room* because "I DON'T SLEEP WITH THE PRESIDENT."

And no, she *won't have* the grand-children's room either. So, she went to the third room, the same dingy room that Ms. Sushma Choudhary was so unhappy about.

A peculiarity of Leh—because of the extreme cold weather was—that there was piped water supply only in the circuit house and the DC's house. But no plumber knew how to do the "mixing" job for the showers. So, the arrangement was that from one tap hot water flowed and from the other cold and both had to be mixed in a bucket before you could have a bath.

There were geysers in all the bathrooms and emergency electricity lines were also arranged from the Alfa Mess of the army which was next door. In the honour of the President new buckets and mugs had been placed in each bathroom. Arun had further got cooks from the army to prepare some South Indian dishes like Idli, Dosa, etc. for the President's breakfast.

The President very graciously invited me and Arun for breakfast. That was when the Lady President dropped the bombshell—that she couldn't have a bath in the morning.

Why? Because there was no "mixing facility" in the shower. And she being a high caste Brahmin couldn't use the buckets. Why? Because they would have sure been used by others and so were deemed "polluted."

The local Congress MP who overheard that lament jumped around and got us *transferred* for "bungling" the President's visit. We hadn't even completed *one year* in Leh.

We wished they could post a plumber as DC Leh and proceeded to pack up.

Chapter 10

Back to the Secretariat

THE TRANSFER FROM Leh did break our heart at one level. However, when I looked at my small child and saw how much he had suffered because of the high altitude, I tried to rationalise. Loss of appetite because of the high altitude, non-availability of fresh fruits and vegetables, the harsh winter when he couldn't be allowed to play outdoors, and the isolation — (no friends of his age because officers didn't keep their families in Leh)—considering all those factors, I felt our pre-mature transfer was, may be, a blessing in disguise.

Many a times Indian Army is compared to the IAS. But when you compare the hardship a civilian officer faces in such areas, there is *no parity*. The army in Leh was fully equipped with winter clothing and shoes, centralised messes for their meals, and all kinds of support systems. The air force would get them fresh vegetables and even "meat-on-hoof" from Agra or Chandigarh. They also had seemingly unlimited supply of all kinds of tinned stuff, including de-hydrated eggs that I was seeing for the first time in my life. They had sufficient man power, unlimited coal and kerosene for space heating and electricity.

And for none of this they had *to pay* a dime. If anything, they were NOT averse to selling their FREE rations, including rum and kerosene, in the open market for a quick buck. Leh in those days had just one petrol pump for the entire district.

But you could go to any village, and openly buy diesel and kerosene from the villagers at rates cheaper than the officially decreed ones, thanks to the "generosity" of the army! As for us poor civilians, we were left to fend for ourselves in our homes at our cost with no infrastructural support from the government.

The Handicrafts Witch Hunt

ON MY RETURN from Leh, I was posted as Additional Secretary Housing and Urban Development, and Arun as Additional Secretary Industry and Commerce. I was pained to see the fate of my favourite projects that I had left behind in the Handicrafts Corporation. For example, the international buyers had placed orders worth Rupees 3-4 crores (30-40 million) on the artisans taking part in the buyers-sellers meet that I had organised.

The Handicrafts Corporation had the responsibility to ensure that goods of the requisite quality were sent on time and payments to the crafts persons were passed on to them smoothly. The export incentive from the Government of India was to come to the corporation as it was registered as a sales and exports corporation. In those days of Licence Raj, this was the only State Public Sector Undertaking permitted to export goods and earn foreign exchange.

Sadly, after I left, none of those commitments was honoured. Many buyers were *infuriated* as they missed out on the Christmas sales they had planned. So, they *blacklisted* the Handicrafts Corporation and swore never to do any business with them again. The local Chamber of Commerce and Industry in Kashmir was gleeful.

"See how useless government corporations are," they chirped.

But things didn't stop there. In fact, a wild witch hunt had been initiated against me which I was blissfully unaware of sitting in Leh. This concerned the J&K stall in the Trade Fair grounds in Delhi that the Handicrafts Corporation was tasked to look after. Mr. Jagmohan didn't like the existing look one bit and desired that I get our stall renovated forthwith. He felt it represented a window to J&K for the millions of visitors coming there and hence must be "presentable."

To do so, I got a list of approved interior designers from the Trade Fair Authority, and invited them to make a presentation. Some 5-6 firms participated and we could finally zero in on one. All procedures and formalities had been followed and the Regional Manager at Delhi, Mr. Shafi, had been fully involved at all stages. The renovation was a roaring success.

But after I and Mr. Jagmohan had departed from the scene, the powers that be—in the J&K Industry and Commerce department—decided to teach me a lesson for espousing the cause of the *downtrodden craftspeople.* They "discovered" that the architect finally chosen was also named Kumar, which was the surname I sport. Although the gentleman was from Kerala, it was made out that I had favoured him because he was *somehow related* to me.

Now to damn me, they needed Mr. Shafi to "cooperate." His job was to *destroy* all records related to this selection so that it could be declared that I had acted in an arbitrary and high handed manner. *I shall be indebted to Mr. Shafi forever who simply refused to oblige.*

In fact, he took out his copy of the Holy Quran and swore that after Allah, he had faith only in me! The negative forces still went ahead and appointed an enquiry officer but nothing could be *proved* and the case against me had to be dropped. *But poor Mr. Shafi—he was harassed so much that he suffered a brain haemorrhage and soon died.*

Taking a Break

WE NEEDED A break rather badly. So, when my only brother, who is 10 years elder to me, invited us to spend some time with him in the US, we happily agreed. In fact, the after effects of living at high altitude in Ladakh was having a terrible effect on our health.

Apparently, our red blood cells had increased manifold to help extract extra oxygen from the rarefied atmosphere. Now that we were back to normal altitudes, the red blood cells had to be slowly destroyed by our bodies. So, we had *low grade fever* continuously that lasted almost six months. We also felt extreme lethargy in doing even the simplest of tasks.

In January 1988, when we got back from the US, we were both posted to Jammu. Arun to a sick, corruption-ridden State Government institution called JAKFED and I as Director Handlooms. Our child was now reaching an age where he needed *formal education*. That was an impossibility with the six-monthly "Darbar Move!"

We, therefore, opted to go to Government of India and by October 1988 Arun had joined the-then Ministry of Energy in the Department of Non-Conventional Energy Sources in New Delhi. Apparently, his work in this sector in Leh was noticed by Mr. Maheshwar Dayal, this Department's Secretary, who had gone out of his way to pick up Arun.

I joined the Ministry of Welfare on the 1st of January 1989. Delhi had its usual shares of accommodation and schooling problems but work wise it was great to be away from J&K. Meanwhile, things were changing rapidly in J&K.

Terrorism hits J&K

THOUGH THINGS seemed peaceful, at one level, there was an undercurrent of unease. The Rajiv-Farooq accord was not doing well. To make matters worse, Government of India decided to import a Chief Secretary from Gujarat, one Mr. Moosa Raza, whose only claim to fame appeared to be that he was a Muslim!

It is strange how such a policy of "appeasement" in J&K, that pleased none, has always proved to be a favourite tool of Government of India. Poor Mr. Moosa Raza. He was clueless about what was happening and was being led up the garden path by the deeply entrenched local officers. So much so that one Mr. Qazi Mohammed Amin, who was junior to me in the IAS, was made a full-fledged Secretary of the General Administration Department (GAD) that dealt with our (and Mr. Amin's) service matters.

While I continued to stew at a lower post as Special Secretary Education. When I protested, and sent a written representation to the Chief Secretary, it was returned with a single line— "The Competent Authority has not acceded to your request." T*hat's all! No explanation whatsoever.*

Amidst all this chaos and confusion, and actually quite in disgust, we left on deputation for Delhi. And shortly thereafter, as if God was just waiting for us to leave, all hell broke loose in J&K. I remember how some craftspeople from Kashmir came to meet me in my office in 1989 and started shedding copious tears (not very unusual for men in Kashmir!) openly.

"Madam, look what has happened to our beautiful Kashmir after you left. As if someone has cursed it. Please come back."

I was stunned for a moment. Yes, Kashmir was cursed. But by none other than us "OUTSIDERS." And that unfortunately included *me.*

Meanwhile things went on taking a turn from bad to worse. Anti-nationalism, communalism and terrorism clutched the whole Kashmir valley in its tight grip. There were selective killings of Kashmiri Pandits, with hit-lists pasted on their doors that led to the exodus of almost the entire Pandit community from Kashmir.

Whole nights, loudspeakers from mosques blared exhorting Muslims to kill "non-believers" which is a euphemism for all non-Muslims. Buses would be stopped in distant Doda and Hindus would be identified, lined up and shot dead. Police with their lathis and .303 World War II-era rifles didn't even know what a Kalashnikov was. Administration simply collapsed.

Mr. Jagmohan who had finished his term was recalled. Immediately, Dr. Farooq Abdullah resigned in protest as he held Mr. Jagmohan responsible for dismissing his government in 1984. The state went under a long spell of Governor's Rule. Mr. Jagmohan tried his best to stem the tide but Mirwaiz Maulvi Farooq's (father of the current Mirwaiz Omar Farooq) assassination and the consequent panicky reaction of the CRPF on the protesters hastened his departure. He was soon replaced by an Army General K.V. Krishna Rao.

All these cataclysmic events were taking place while we were in Delhi. We were happy to put our son in the infant class of DPS (Delhi Public School) Vasant Vihar/R.K. Puram the moment he turned four.

But our four-year tenure with the Government of India ended as if in the blink of an eye. And in March 1993, we had to return very reluctantly to the ugly boiling cauldron of J&K.

Chapter 11

My Trips to Pakistan

THE DAWN OF 1989 saw me joining my first posting in Government of India as a Deputy Secretary in the Ministry of Welfare. This was a huge ministry at that time and included the subjects of disability, tribal welfare, welfare of scheduled caste and minorities, juvenile justice, and drug abuse prevention. Nowadays almost each of these subjects is handled by a separate department in the Government of India.

I was assigned the drug abuse prevention division. The Secretary Mr. S.S. Verma told me he had personally picked me up as he found my profile to be ideally suited for the job. He added with a twinkle in his eyes that he wanted a "high flying" officer with varied experience who could bring a fresh perspective to this important division.

1989 had been declared as the SAARC year against *drug abuse*. The pictures of Rajiv Gandhi and Benazir Bhutto, raising their hands together in support of this mission were splashed everywhere.

Drug abuse prevention pivots around two broad aspects: Checking the production, supply and sale of narcotics on one hand, and to stem the demand for such drugs on the other. I was the nodal officer for the latter, the demand reduction aspects. An empowered committee was created under Secretary Welfare with the Secretary Health and Family Welfare and Joint Secretary Prime Minister's Office as members. This committee was authorised to create posts and sanction funds for this programme.

In my very first meeting and presentation to this committee, I was sanctioned five additional posts and the budget of my division was tripled.

Foreign trip opportunities were galore; so much so I had to start declining them. In that sense, mine was indeed a very "high-flying" division!

Of course, this meant a lot of hard work as it was already January and funds were to be utilised by the end of March.

One interesting aspect of my job was that I had to deal with several non-governmental organisations (NGOs) working for this cause. Funds were mostly meant for encouraging their involvement and not for distribution to the State Governments as was the case with most other Government of India projects.

I started with 28 NGOs and within a short time we crossed the one hundred mark. By the time, I left Government of India, there were over 363 NGOs working for this sector spread throughout the length and breadth of the country.

We produced information material and also laid down the protocol to be followed in de-addiction centres. The NGOs were also to do follow-ups so that the de-addicts did not "relapse" i.e. fall back into addiction.

My Secretary was ecstatic with my work. He told me that officers consider a posting in the Commerce Ministry great because they can then go on a number of foreign visits. He said he would ensure that I had the same privilege of going abroad in the Ministry of Welfare as often as I wished. And he stuck to his promise.

Anti-India Everywhere

THE FIRST OFFICIAL foreign visit I made was to—Islamabad, Pakistan in April 1989. There was a SAARC meeting of NGOs in Islamabad and I had to lead the Indian delegation.

After getting the first official passport of my life, the External Affairs Ministry got the visa to Pakistan stamped. When I got the passport in my hands, I was surprised to see the visa saying "Valid for Islamabad only." It next added that "I was exempted from reporting to the police station."

It was then I learnt that India and Pakistan had this peculiar practice of giving each other's nationals a "city-specific" visa unlike other governments where a visa is valid for the whole country for whatever period one pays the visa fee for.

Another fact I learnt to my surprise was that there were NO international flights to Islamabad although it is the capital of Pakistan. We had to land at Lahore, complete our immigration formalities and then take a "domestic flight" to Islamabad.

At Islamabad, we were received properly and taken to our hotel. I always had an armed escort with me which was supposedly for ensuring my safety but *was actually* to keep an eye on who I was meeting.

The conference began as all conferences do and all seemed to be going well as planned. We were even taken for some sight-seeing to the Faisal mosque and other tourist places in Islamabad. Since I was representing India, I always made a point to wear a sari and sport a *bindi* (the sticker that many Indian women wear on their foreheads). That didn't go too well with the locals as I noticed a few burqa clad women near the Faisal mosque lifting their veil and giving me a *hostile stare.*

We were also taken to Murree, the so-called hill-station of Pakistan. I found it a terrible disappointment as it looked like any other insignificant hill town that India is dotted with. Like say, Solan in Himachal Pradesh! However, it was considered grand by Pakistani standards. In fact, one of our escorting officials asked me whether we had any hill-stations at all in India!

So much for their general knowledge! I also realised that an average Pakistani is NOT well-travelled as he is NOT encouraged to go beyond the *boundaries of his province.*

Another strange incident took place in Murree. There were a group of young girls wearing *Salwaar Kameez* (the normal dress for Punjabi women) who suddenly looked at me and shouted, *"Arre ye toh Ram Ram hai!"* Meaning "Oh this one is from the (damned) land of Lord Rama."

I lost my cool and asked them whether they had any manners or *"tameez"* as they call it in Urdu in Pakistan and whether this was what they were taught in colleges. That put them in their places and shut them up. Later as my escorts sheepishly admitted—this was the exact kind of poison against India—that Pakistani textbooks were bringing up their kids on.

A weird question everyone used to ask me was, "From which part of Pakistan did your ancestors go to India?"

This—I was told was a compliment to my fair complexion! But I had to disappoint them by saying that none of my ancestors had ventured anywhere near Pakistan as I belong to Bihar, in Eastern India!

This seemed to have quite a freezing effect. The word "Bihar" used to take away their smiles— because most of the trouble-making "Mohajirs" or outsiders in Pakistan, came from there.

The local markets were full of all kinds of imported stuff. One person proudly informed me that the milk they were supplying to our hotel was imported from Denmark. I was *aghast* and thankful that we had our own home-grown Amul everywhere.

I was, however, interested in knowing what the local handicrafts and handlooms were. So, I was taken to a government emporium which was supposed to represent the whole of Pakistan. The place was disappointingly small—it was equal in size to just one state emporium of J&K at Delhi's Baba Kharak Singh Marg. After much looking around I could pick up only an onyx lamp with a camel skin shade. Unlike Kashmir, the handicrafts industry was certainly not thriving in Pakistan.

The dependence on American aid revealed itself when an official in Pakistan asked me whether we had *computers* in my office.

"Of course," I said.

The next question was whether those computers were given to us by the *Amriki* (US) Government.

I clarified that they were all locally manufactured and had been supplied by my own government. One of them then sighed and remarked to his colleague, "*Arey Mian*, these guys are not dependent on the US for everything as we are."

To Peshawar "Without Permission"

THERE WAS A day's break before we could take a flight back home. An NGO from Pakistan insisted that we utilise that break to visit his home in Peshawar.

But it was NOT that easy to accept such an invitation. The problem was that my visa, as I mentioned, was "city-specific" only for Islamabad. So, I asked the Pakistan Foreign Service guy who was there in the meeting if I could go to Peshawar. By evening I was informed that my request couldn't be acceded to.

When I discussed this problem with the NGO, a true blue *Pathan*, he exploded. He said his mother was so keen to meet us Indians and he couldn't disappoint her. He suggested that I should forget "these Punjabis" i.e. the ruling classes, and just come with him.

What I had to do simply—was to wear a *Salwar Kameez*, cover my head and not wear a *bindi*! Rest he would take care of. The foolhardy person I am, I agreed reluctantly.

So, next morning, in Islamabad, the NGO's car with his personal security guard came early, before my Pakistani escorts had arrived, and I slipped out. The drive to Peshawar through the rugged landscape was unbelievable.

The road was smooth but after we left Islamabad, there seemed to be NO development anywhere along the highway.

Nothing seemed to grow on either side of the road. We crossed *Taxila*, the historic university town of ancient India, where *Chanakya* once taught *Chandragupta* in 300 BC, and which is now an army cantonment. From a distance, I saw what looked like an abandoned temple with the head of the goddess missing.

Peshawar was a dusty medieval town selling a lot of dry fruits in the open. It almost seemed I had travelled back in time by a few centuries. My host's house, however, was a sprawling modern structure with exquisite wooden carvings and at least five bedrooms. His mother hugged me as if I was some long lost relative. She told me how she loved Indians and Afghans and hated the Punjabi Pakistanis.

"See our tragedy," she said. "We have been separated from the two nations and people we love the most."

My host also drove me to a point on the outskirts of Peshawar from where I could see the outlines of the Khyber Pass. *En route* we came across a camp of Afghan refugees which was a frightening experience. Most had one or two limbs missing. The women were all begging. Bearded men were carrying *deadly looking firearms*.

They could all so easily pass for the *gujjar* and *bakerwal nomads* of J&K. I felt a shiver go down my spine when I thought what havoc could be created if these guys ever infiltrated into Kashmir.

Little did I know that my premonition was going to come true so soon. It was April 1989 then, and just a few months thereafter, in December 1989, havoc was indeed let loose in Kashmir.

When we returned to Islamabad from our adventure in the evening, I found some agitated security personnel in the hotel lobby.

"Madam, where have you been?"

I smiled and said, "Mostly sleeping in my room! And taking some small walks."

The Pakistanis glared at me—but backed off as—trying to prove that I had cheated on their city-specific visa would have only exposed their negligence!

Dealing with Mr. Krishnan

1989 SOON CAME to an end and with it came the end of the Rajiv Gandhi government. In 1990, Mr. V.P. Singh became the prime minister. Sitting in the Welfare Ministry, one felt the tremors of implementing the Mandal Commission Report which gave reservation to a newly coined category called "Other Backward Classes" or OBCs. The dormant caste lines were suddenly re-ignited with a ferocity that shocked us all. There were self-immolations and riots galore everywhere.

Mr. S.S. Verma, my Secretary, also retired in December 1989. Thereafter we had all kinds of secretaries with shorter and shorter tenures.

Mr. V.P. Singh soon lost his majority in the Parliament and in came Mr. Chandra Shekhar. The whole country continued to be in turmoil. The changes in the government were felt most keenly in the subjects I was dealing with. They suddenly lost the focus and priority they once enjoyed.

Drug abuse prevention became such a non-issue that a Secretary named Mr. P.S. Krishnan declared rather proudly in a conference of NGOs that he *knew nothing* about drug abuse as no one *was* consuming drugs in his family! He further opined that the problem arose because of the "rat race" prevalent in the modern society where the whole family were like *rats*.

Mr. Krishnan then went on to add that the subject was so obtuse or irrelevant that it was only officers like "Sonali Kumar" who knew something about it!

That was too much. I had to correct him then and there. So, I took the mike and told my secretary:

"Sorry Sir. Even in my family no one consumes drugs or smokes cigarettes or even drinks alcohol. Fighting drug-addiction is just a job entrusted to me by the government that

I am trying to discharge to the best of my abilities. And if the government wants that I do something else, I shall be most happy to attend to that."

There was a stunned silence for a moment and then the entire hall erupted with a thunderous applause. In the audience, there were many recovering addicts who had dedicated their lives to helping others. They obviously agreed with me much more and—realising their mood Mr. Krishnan was forced to shut up.

You can imagine the consequences of such a publicly made "correction" on my Annual Performance Reports! And on my career!

Working with Mr. Sitaram Kesari

STABILITY RETURNED to India only after Mr. P.V. Narasimha Rao became the Prime Minister. Mr. Sitaram Kesari was allotted the welfare portfolio. In the first interaction I had with him, I had to contradict him a little as he thought the problem of drug abuse affected only the well-to-do. I had the facts and figures to show that all classes were equally affected and — in fact in the less affluent—it was also linked with crimes. On the whole, drug abuse was a disease which affected all, and the entire family, be they rich or poor.

Unlike Mr. Krishnan, Mr. Kesari somehow liked my spunk and started trusting me more and more. Besides drug abuse prevention, he assigned me the job of publicity and awareness building for all the subjects (and NOT just drug abuse prevention) being dealt by the ministry with a huge budget.

Dealing with the media is always tricky. So, I had laid down set procedures, norms, and criteria to make the selection of films and advertisements very transparent. I generally had no problems but then there were always exceptions.

One day I got a call that the minister wanted me to meet him in his office in Parliament sharp at 4 p.m. I had no idea why I had been called and when I asked his personal secretary, he said he too had no clue.

I reached the Parliament a few minutes before 4 and saw Mr. Kesari sitting behind a huge office table. He acknowledged my greetings and motioned me to sit on the sofa which was placed at the other end of the room.

Sharp at 4, Mr. Kesari came to my side and occupied a single-seater sofa. Immediately thereafter a fat lady straddled in followed by a film maker. I recognised the latter right away as I had only recently rejected the film he had produced because of some serious deficiencies.

The film maker waved his hands frantically trying to warn the lady Member of Parliament (MP) about my presence but the lady couldn't see all that commotion as she was marching ahead. Soon she sat down and started,

"Kesari ji, you have a Deputy Secretary who has really been troubling people (*naak mein dum karke rakha hai* to be more precise)." And thus, she delivered her full prepared speech.

Mr. Kesari heard the MP out patiently and then asked,

"Do you know this Deputy Secretary?"

When the lady shook her head to indicate she didn't, he turned around and said, "Here she is."

Then he asked, "Yes Sonali, what is the case?"

As the whole file flashed in my brain, I thanked God for blessing me with an excellent memory. I explained in detail the money that had already been released to the film maker and the kind of shoddy product he had then come up with. Mr. Kesari turned to the film maker and in a stern voice told him, "You've heard what you have to do! Do it, and even after that, if your funds are held up, then come to me. Now you can leave."

The film maker left and then Mr. Kesari turned to the lady, "Madam you are a Congress MP. If you need money come to me, come to Sitaram Kesari All India Congress Committee Treasurer. But don't come just like that looking for money from my ministry and also criticise my *best* officer in the process."

The lady apologised and left red-faced. And then Mr. Kesari said something which I shall always remember:

"Sonali you are an excellent and a very bold officer. In your life, many people will try to frighten and bamboozle you. But always remember this advice of an old man—stick to your stand and never get scared."

And I vowed to act on that advice regardless of the consequences to my career in the IAS!

A Second Trip to Pakistan

AS THE NODAL officer for drug abuse prevention, I was also assigned the job of Project Coordinator for India, for an International Labour Organization (ILO) initiative for drug abuse prevention in the South Asia (SAARC) region. In this connection, I had to visit Islamabad one more time.

This time, I was going alone. The bookings had all been done by the ILO office in Delhi.

My hotel was in Rawalpindi which is a twin town of Islamabad. The crowded marketplaces reminded me of old Delhi except that there were a lot of army vehicles moving on the road. The discussions in the ILO meeting gave us a view of the drug and arms availability in Pakistan. The work being done in India was appreciated by all especially the ILO head of drug abuse prevention who was an Iranian based in Geneva. After the official meeting was over, I was seen off by the local hosts at the Islamabad Airport.

My return journey to India had been booked very peculiarly by the travel agent of ILO. My flight was to go from Islamabad to Lahore and then to Karachi. From Karachi, I was to take the PIA (Pakistan International Airlines) flight back to Delhi.

As luck would have it, my flight from Islamabad developed a technical snag and was terminated at Lahore. I tried my best to convince the PIA staff to accommodate me on a flight going from Lahore to New Delhi but they flatly refused. I was told

I could either go back to Islamabad or to Karachi when all I wanted was to get back home.

Once while going to US, our PANAM flight had stopped for a while in Karachi. So, I thought lots of airlines operated on the Karachi-New Delhi sector. I was desperately looking for alternatives because I had already missed my original flight on PIA from Karachi to New Delhi.

So, around 8 PM, I agreed to get on a flight headed for Karachi. I asked the air hostess that since I had now missed my PIA flight to New Delhi if there could be any other flight I could take to go to Delhi. She looked at me and asked, "Are you an Indian?"

When I nodded my head, she said, "Well, then you can only fly PIA or Air India and there are no flights today."

That was the arrangement between India and Pakistan for their nationals!

I felt as though I was struck by a lightning. Here I was, flying alone to Karachi, at such late hours, where I didn't know a soul.

I didn't even have the number of the Indian Consulate there and these were not the days when you could have mobile phones. In fact, back in my ministry, I had heard that because of the terrible law and order situation in Karachi no Indian diplomatic staff *dared* venture out at night.

So, what was I to do except pray. I had never felt more miserable in my life. The plane landed, and we slowly moved towards the ladder to deplane.

I think God took pity on me because suddenly a man wearing a *Pathan* suit looked at me and pointed to the left, and said,

"You from India? Go there, they'll help you!"

And then he disappeared in the crowd.

There is a saying that for a drowning man even a floating twig gives some hope. So blindly I walked in the indicated direction and reached a rather well-decorated tent. As soon as

I stepped in, I was greeted effusively. I was escorted to a sofa and cold drinks and salted cashew nuts were proffered.

After gathering my wits, I told my hosts how I had missed my flight to Delhi.

"Don't worry madam, we'll take care of everything!"

But how had I become a VIP?

I looked around and saw a signboard which read, "Entrepreneurs Welcome to Pakistan!"

I learnt that the Director Industries of Karachi had been stationed at the Karachi Airport to look after industrialists who had been invited from all over the world to invest in Pakistan. And that conference too was being held in Islamabad around the same time that mine was. So, in my silk sari, I was taken as some tycoon who had come from India to invest in Pakistan!

I got chatting with the director and realised how his service matters, disregarding seniorities, and the general functioning of his department were so similar to the chaos we had in J&K. If Kashmiris ever went under the jackboots of the Punjabi Pakistanis, they would sorely miss the impartiality and professionalism we "outsiders" bring to Kashmir, I mused. Of course, I never revealed my true identity or my connections with Kashmir.

I had to wait till my tickets were reissued for the next day. It was almost 11 p.m. when a hotel could be arranged and I could be taken to that in a Toyota. I remember the brand because this was not yet available in India. My hosts were so gracious that they even arranged for me to speak to my husband in India—who was very calm little realising the deep sh*t I was in.

Karachi looked *haunted* especially as many houses had bullet marks on them.

The hotel had a funny notice stuck on my room's door. It read, "If a woman is staying alone, no man is allowed to enter her room!"

I was too tired to either laugh or raise my eyebrows and just crashed.

I spent the next day locked up in my hotel room till my hosts came and escorted me to the Karachi Airport. I could finally leave for New Delhi.

My eyes filled with tears when I saw the lights at the Indira Gandhi International Airport.

I was so happy to get back!

The ILO was so happy with my handling of their project that they invited me to Vienna as an expert on drug abuse prevention and put me in an expert group to work out the next decade's plan for the UN. I was even offered a job with the ILO in Geneva but I had to decline as I didn't want to leave my family in India.

Our term in Government of India came to an end in December 1992 and after availing of some leave— I and Arun were both back in J&K by early 1993.

Chapter 12

Suffering "Army Rule" in J&K

WHEN WE LANDED back in J&K in March 1993, we couldn't recognise the place. J&K had changed so much, and mostly for the worse. The place was crawling with security personnel who peeped from every nook and corner. Jammu town still felt the same but most of Kashmir was out of bounds for all civilians, including officers like us.

Since I had a small 9-year-old who needed to go to school, I requested for a "non-move" Jammu based posting and was made Director of Handlooms. That must be the least important (and least lucrative) posting from the point of view of the powers that be.

I noted wistfully how in my Senior Scale of pay in the IAS, six years back, I was the MD Handicrafts, Sales & Exports Corporation and Director Handicrafts. Later in my Junior Administrative Grade, I was Director Handlooms and MD of the Handloom Development Corporation. But now in my Selection Grade of the IAS, I was only Director Handlooms—full stop! Anyway, I couldn't protest as I had myself asked for a Jammu posting.

J&K was under Governor's rule and the Governor was General Krishna Rao who had been once upon a time—Chief of the Indian Army. Krishna Rao may have been a great General but was clueless about civil administration. So, while he focussed on tackling the law and order issues with the army and the para-military, he left the civil administration totally in the hands of Sheikh Ghulam Rasool, my old *bête noir*, who was now the Chief Secretary.

The "Legend" that was Sheikh Ghulam Rasool

SHEIKH GHULAM RASOOL had joined the local Kashmir Administrative Service (KAS) through the backdoor (i.e. without getting through any open entrance examination) in 1964. So typical of J&K.

He soon managed to get himself posted to the General Administrative Department (GAD), that looks after the service matters of all employees, and thereafter remained in that department for 10 long years, rising to the post of Secretary. The result was that he could not only get himself promoted to the IAS but could also fix his year of allotment as 1965! He was the new evil sorcerer!

So virtually after just *one year* of service in the local feeding service like the KAS, he had been promoted to the IAS which was, dubious as it may be, an all-India record! And now he was the Chief Secretary.

"How is that possible?" my colleagues in other states exclaimed in horror. BUT this is J&K and in trying to appease the state cadre officers, the Government of India, in those days used to play along, trampling upon the rights of us direct recruit *outsiders* mercilessly. Anything and everything was possible at the altar of "national interest" in J&K, especially the *impossible*.

Or the unthinkable.

I had had no love lost for Sheikh Ghulam Rasool from day 1 of my service in J&K. Rasool had been my first boss as Agricultural Production Commissioner where he had given me NO work. Later also, he continued to dislike me for what I represented, which in my sari and bindi attire meant "Indianness."

Or *Bharatiyata* that people of his ilk detested deeply.

Anyway, I was happy with my current work in Handlooms and went about it quite seriously. I took extra effort to guide and groom the officers who were working as my Assistant Directors in the Handlooms Department. I gave them excellent performance reports and got them promoted at the right time. This not only enthused them but also enabled them to hold important positions in the government in many other departments.

The greatest enthusiasm at my posting was from the weavers and craftspeople of Kashmir. I had dealt with them earlier in my previous postings in the Handicrafts and the Handlooms departments and they were thrilled at my coming back to the sector.

Arun Inventing Work as Secretary Ladakh Affairs

THE SECRETARIAT shifted to Srinagar at the end of April 1993. Arun was made Secretary of the Ladakh Affairs Department, an inconsequential post that Rasool had especially carved out from the Tourism Department just for Arun to *rot* in. That also meant that Arun had to move to Srinagar in May leaving me and our son behind in Jammu.

I could go on my first official tour to Srinagar sometime in June. The scenario was unbelievable. No one was living in any of the official houses that we once had in colonies like Tulsibagh, Jawahar Nagar or Sonwar. Instead, all senior officers were now housed in single rooms in the Centaur Hotel on the banks of the Dal Lake. Two meals a day were provided—breakfast and dinner—in a common mess or dining hall.

There was no freedom of movement. You couldn't go anywhere: to the market, to a friend's house, for weddings or for sight-seeing. No personal or official vehicles were permitted. All Secretaries had to get into a bus in the morning and like *prisoners* escorted by armed police to the Secretariat. And similarly return in the evening.

Most of the time no supporting staff would turn up, not even the cleaning staff. So, I found Arun carrying the keys to his office room that he would open himself, dust it a bit, do some policy-related work which he could do without files, and lock the room back when returning to the hotel in the evenings. No files moved anywhere. Lunch boxes were banned. So, for lunch, J&K Tourism Development Corporation served vegetarian soup with toast—on *payment*, of course.

Arun tried his best to keep himself busy by thinking of new proposals for Ladakh. The one for creating a *Leh Festival* on fixed dates from September 1-15 every year (because all other monastery-related festivals are NOT held on fixed dates) was accepted by the Tourism Department headed by its super-enthusiastic Secretary Parvez Dewan. This festival continues to be held on these dates, which otherwise is the "lean season" for Leh, EVEN TODAY.

The other proposal that could revolutionise the tourism sector in Leh related to the opening of the "motorable route" to Mansarovar Lake and Mount Kailash in Tibet via Demchok in Leh District. Hindu pilgrims then could take a one-hour flight from Delhi to Leh, acclimatise for a day, and then take a bus for a two-day journey over some 400 odd kilometres to Mansarovar. The existing roads were excellent, except for a 200-metre rough patch in a "no-man's-land" across Demchok. There were no high altitude passes on the way, and so pilgrims could go to Mansarovar in all seasons, round the year, if they so wished.

Arun pursued the proposal relentlessly with all the limited resources at his command. First, he was asked to submit a route map, including where in Tibet pilgrims could camp. This he managed through his sources in the Indo-Tibetan Border Police (ITBP).

Then the Ministry of External Affairs stonewalled the idea on the ground that going through Demchok would mean India opening an Immigration post in an area where borders are disputed, thus diluting Indian claims over that area! What this meant for Indian pilgrims/tourists, who were dying in hundreds over the existing route through Uttar Pradesh (now Uttarakhand) hills, was of no consequence. No wonder, this proposal couldn't see the light of the day even till now.

The third idea related to the formation of a Hill Council in Leh, on the pattern of the one in Darjeeling. Sheikh Ghulam Rasool wanted the powers of the proposed council reduced drastically and was not happy that Arun, as an old Ladakh hand, was not "co-operating." Any way the council had so much political support at the local level that it did become a reality despite all odds.

Working with Kashmiri Crafts Persons AGAIN

I COULD STAY with Arun in the Centaur Hotel. But it was a total house arrest for me and my son. And yes, no lunch could be provided to us too, for love or for money.

I had sent information to my Joint Director Handlooms to come to Centaur for a meeting. But what actually happened was unbelievable. As the clock struck 10 in the morning, a crowd slowly started building up outside the gates of the hotel. The CRPF (Central reserve Police Force) DSP (Deputy Superintendent of Police) in charge of security rushed in and told me that the crowd had come to meet me claiming they were all weavers and craftspeople. He wanted to know whether I could identify them.

I said no, I couldn't, but if they had come to meet me, I'll meet them. The DSP could search them as much as he liked but if I was NOT allowed to go to my office, which was outside the Secretariat and hence "unsafe," I had no option but to meet them in the hotel.

So, after 2-3 rounds of heavy frisking, the weavers were allowed to come in. Since the hotel had no functioning conference or office room, where I could meet them, we sat on the lawns under the majestic Chinar trees and held our meeting. I was touched beyond words.

It was only because of my previous association with this sector that I had this tremendous response. I discussed various schemes and programmes with the craftsmen and realised that maybe mine was one of the few departments which could function in the field even during those troubled times.

Many of the weavers were from downtown Srinagar which was the *hotbed* of terrorism. Nonetheless, some suggested that they could get a boat and I could come with them to their homes for a meal or at least some warm cups of *Kehwa* as I was like a daughter/sister to them.

The DSP, who was standing hawk-eyed during all this talk, protested at this "sinister" suggestion. He said, and I had to agree reluctantly, that "foreigners," meaning Pakistanis, had taken over the area and that they did not believe in *any* relationship except that of the gun. Kidnapping me or killing me, a lady IAS officer, would make *good news* for them and that was all they were interested in. So, the foolhardy idea was nipped in the bud!

I couldn't, however, restrain myself from discussing "azadi" with the craftspeople and asked them whether they really wanted "outsider" officers like me to leave J&K *forever*. The shock and horror that their faces reflected was unbelievable.

No, no! Very rarely do we get such good officers, they protested. Left to Kashmiris, we would just be "gobbled up."

"Then what do you want?"

That got them chatting. Someone said *azadi* meant getting rid of Farooq Abdullah permanently! Another wanted jobs for their kin *on merit* without greasing any palms. Others wanted freedom to travel anywhere without being subjected to frisking, roadblocks or curfews.

In essence, what they all wanted was a toning down of the security apparatus and a *just and fair* administration for all—and not appeasement for the top 3% of the population which was what the Government of India indulged in. And continues to do so even till this date. That was *alienating* the remaining 97% who were then forced to pick up the gun, some opined.

Soon regardless of the disturbed conditions, I had to become busier and busier in my little department. At one end, I was trying to get pictures of pashmina designs from museums in London, as the originals had been lost in Kashmir, and getting these duplicated. On the other, I was trying to take pashmina and *Kani/Jamawar* shawl weaving and embroidery to another level with rural tourism to the village Kanihama where *Kani* shawl weaving was still being practised.

The only thing I was not willing to support was the use of *shahtoosh,* which is the softest and the most expensive wool in the world. It comes from a wild goat called *Chiru* found in the high-altitude areas of Ladakh. Till I went to Leh, I had believed in the Kashmiri stories that *shahtoosh* was obtained when the *Chiru* rubbed itself on stones and bushes and left its wool behind.

Once in Leh, I learnt to my horror that getting *shahtoosh* was not at all a *non-violent* natural activity. In fact, to get these, you had to shoot down hundreds of *Chirus,* skin them and then comb the fine wool out. Naturally, the wild life conservationists were up against this cruel practice and prevailed upon Government of India to ban the use of *shahtoosh.* That did hit the Kashmiri craftsmen rather hard. But since skills of weaving *shahtoosh* or *pashmina* are similar, the workers in due course switched over to pashmina weaving totally.

However, the middlemen used to their skyrocketing profits on the trade of *shahtoosh* didn't like the ban one bit. They were supported in this by people like Sheikh Ghulam Rasool who even prevailed upon the Governor to write a letter to the Government of India requesting that they lift the ban. I could, however, NOT support that move in any forum and that too put me directly in to the cross hairs of Mr. Rasool.

Regardless I was trying to work with national level fashion designers to help open new markets for our handloom products. But in J&K you can never work peacefully, can you?

Crossing Swords with Sheikh Ghulam Rasool

MR. RASOOL, the Chief Secretary, even otherwise did not like the fact that I was happy and satisfied in a department which most officers considered a *dumping* ground. So, something had to be done to unnerve me.

The State Government sometime back had created a "Women Development Corporation" under the Social Welfare Department which was headed by Pradeep K. Tripathi (IAS 1987), then-Additional Secretary in the Governor's Secretariat. Pradeep was transferred as DC Leh and the Chief Secretary ordered that his charge be handled by me (eight years his senior!) in addition to my duties.

Nothing wrong with this (according to Mr. Rasool) except that then I'd be forced to *report* to Secretary Social Welfare Mrs. Vijay Kotwal, a promoted IAS officer, who was *junior* to me in the IAS.

So, I met the Chief Secretary to register my reservations, but he refused to even listen. Instead he *threatened* that if I didn't "behave" he will open some old cases against me from the time I was MD Handicrafts Corporation. He apparently had forgotten how he had tried so hard when he headed the Industry Department then but had failed to indict me.

And then Mr. Rasool asked me very superciliously, "And you know who I am?"

I said, "Yes sir. You are the Chief Secretary and the most powerful Chief Secretary this state has ever known."

Mr. Rasool glared at me. So, I added,

"But sir I also have two things with me."

He looked at me surprised. What could I, an *outsider*, with no local godfathers possibly have?

"And that is, Sir, courage in my heart and God above."

The meeting was over. But Mr. Rasool was fuming. He immediately made out a case for placing me under *suspension* for "defying government orders." It was another matter that in J&K many a times officers were refusing to take up even substantial postings if it were not to their liking. But in my case, a big hue and cry, was being made over a mere additional charge.

I tried to meet the Governor but was told by Mr. Rajnath, his Personal Secretary that the great General *didn't like* to meet junior officers. His Secretary Mr. S.S. Bloeria, however, heard me out and advised that I *don't fight* with Mr. Rasool. His remark was:

"When you live in a pond, you don't mess with crocodiles."

Not one to accept defeat, I then tried to reach out to the Cabinet Secretary in the Government of India in Delhi. The gentleman too had no time for us *lowly creatures*. Then I learnt he was a great friend of the Chief Secretary on account of the lavish *gifts* that the latter used to shower on him.

Apparently, the Cabinet Secretary was told that the beautiful shawls his wife had received were embroidered by the Chief Secretary's mother, the exquisite Kashmiri silk carpets were woven by the latter's sister, and the crates of apples were, of course, from Mr. Rasool's own family orchard.

Funnily, even today when senior Government of India officers receive such gifts from Kashmiri officers, they are told similar stories of how skilled the latter's family members are!

I felt foolish and terribly alone in my quest to establish the principles I believed in. Only Arun, my husband, kept my morale high and prevented me from going in to deep depression.

Just then, I thought God heard my silent prayers. Suddenly, two new advisors to the Governor came to be appointed by the Government of India: Mr. Moses and Mr. Murshid. Mr. Moses had gone to the Ministry of Welfare as Secretary just after I had left and had apparently heard a lot of good words from the NGOs who had worked with me closely. He was keen to meet me and was extremely positive towards me.

Mr. Murshid was a retired officer of the West Bengal cadre who I didn't have the pleasure of meeting ever. But he was now the Governor's advisor for Industries and Commerce and thus my "minister" for all practical purposes. So, willy-nilly I started having many official reviews, meetings and interactions with him.

An interesting factor I have noted in my career, as also in my social/personal life, is that—people either love me or hate me. I have yet to come across anyone who is neutral in his views about what I do or don't do. I wonder why?

Anyway, to my relief, both advisers took a great liking to me. One day I got a phone call from Mr. Murshid asking me to come to his office immediately. As soon as I entered his room, he handed me a file. The file had that noting of the Chief Secretary, that I was dreading for quite some time. It was about seeking the approval of the Governor for placing me under *suspension* for gross defiance of government orders.

Now Mr. Murshid was also in-charge of the GAD. So the file had to come to him before being submitted to the Governor. Mr. Murshid had recorded that he considered me an outstanding officer. Also, that in the IAS (as also in the army or the police), no officer reports to a *junior* and so by refusing to do so, I was exhibiting "no defiance." If the nascent Women Corporation (that was still on paper with neither any office nor staff) needed an MD, Mr. Murshid suggested, the Secretary Social Welfare could herself hold the charge.

"Governor may please approve," he suggested in the end.

The Governor had approved, and the file was on its way back when Mr. Murshid so magnanimously (and mischievously?) showed it to me.

But Mr. Murshid couldn't hide his curiosity. He asked me why the Chief Secretary *disliked* me so much. That did it.

All my pent-up anger and frustration of the past two-three months burst out in the open. I explained how that was because we were completely on two opposing sides of the spectrum. I take great pride in my honesty, integrity and loyalty for India and the Indian Constitution. And, of course, he was just the opposite.

I added how my room is open to all and how I had Kashmiri friends at various levels. It was they who had told me all kinds of stories about Mr. Rasool. That he had got his son appointed through the back door in to JAKFED—a loss-making State Government organisation and then surreptitiously into the Kashmir Administrative Service. That he had given shelter to a Deputy Commissioner of Anantnag District who was actually a BDO (Block Development Officer). This officer had put Rupees fourteen crores (140 million) of Government of India *money* in his personal bank account and when caught absconded with his driver, Personal Security Officer and official vehicle to hide in Mr. Rasool's official residence. Also, how Rasool was so thick with the anti-India and pro-Pakistan Hurriyat, whose meetings were also being held in Mr. Rasool's official residence.

I narrated all these tit-bits to Mr. Murshid and requested him to get these *verified* through the intelligence agencies. He did exactly that and to his horror found these to be 100% true.

As an old-world bureaucrat, Mr. Murshid took it all up very seriously with the Government of India. Meanwhile the Cabinet Secretary, who was almost in Rasool's pockets, retired and his successor decided to go along with Mr. Murshid to ask Sheikh Ghulam Rasool to either *quit* or *face consequences*.

Surprisingly, Rasool chose to retire voluntarily, creating no fuss, and that too almost one year *before* his due date of retirement. This was unheard of in the annals of J&K bureaucracy. *The God above and the courage in my heart had indeed won.* My phone wouldn't stop ringing as I was flooded with congratulatory messages from all over Kashmir.

But taking on such a mighty adversary took its toll on poor Mr. Murshid. Rasool's benefactors hit back dubbing Mr. Murshid as "anti-Kashmir." Shortly thereafter he was removed as advisor. How can Government of India do such a foolish thing? But they did.

Revising Seniorities Once Again

THE NEW CHIEF Secretary was Mr. HH Tyabji (IAS 1965), an affable mild mannered person from a hoary family background. I had had excellent relations with him at the time I had worked under him as Deputy Secretary PWD in 1981. However, this had soured during the Governor's rule under Mr. Jagmohan who used to deal with me directly, ignoring Mr. Tyabji.

During one of my tours to the valley, I got invited, along with other senior officers, to have dinner with the Principal Secretary to the PM, Mr. Venugopal who was on an official visit to Srinagar. I knew Mr. Venugopal from the days he was the Joint Secretary Women and Child Development while I was Deputy Secretary in the Welfare Department. Our rooms were adjacent to each other in Shastri Bhavan New Delhi and we would almost every day bump into each other in the corridors and exchange pleasantries.

The dinner was at the picturesque Centaur Hotel. At the appointed time, Mr. Venugopal came with a big smile and grandly announced that he had got the Prime Minister's nod to over-rule the objections of the Central Department of Personnel to the new seniority list of the IAS officers in J&K. When the news sank in, we were shocked beyond words.

This meant that some local promotee officers who had been junior to me for the last ten years would become my senior! The batch of a direct recruit officer like me is like an albatross which hangs around our necks till we die. But promoted officers—can they keep getting their years of allotment to the IAS changed at the sweet will of powers that be?

I couldn't restrain myself and walked up to Mr. Venugopal. I asked him if he could spare two minutes. Venugopal was in an expansive mood, and said,

"Why Sonali, why two minutes? You can have as much time as you want."

"Because, sir," I replied, "What I am going to say, you will *not be* able to hear for more than two minutes."

Mr. Venugopal came aside but Mr. Qazi Mohammed Amin who was one of the beneficiaries of this seniority-revision order intruded to stop me. But I had made up my mind. So, I started with the background of the whole seniority mess as it obtained in J&K and gave Mr. Venugopal the example of Mr. Amin himself.

I explained that when I was posted as MD Handicrafts in 1986, I was no doubt holding an important post but the post was officially not one of the "cadre posts" of the IAS. Mr. Amin at the same time was made Deputy Commissioner Srinagar, a "cadre post" without figuring anywhere in either the IAS or in the "Select List" for promotion to the IAS.

Then I was packed off as Director Desert Development Leh, again a "non-cadre" post while Amin was made Director Industries—a cadre post. Similarly, when I became Director Handlooms—a non-cadre post, he was made the Secretary GAD. Now because he went on holding "cadre posts" *illegally* that I or any other IAS officer of my seniority should have held, Government of India had decided to *reward* him by making him my senior! And that also when all along till that time I had treated him as my junior.

And then I added,

"Sir, do you want to know the cause of militancy in J&K?... It is because of those tears of us direct recruits that flow because of the grave injustice that the local and the central government together heap on us."

That was all. Mr. Venugopal was too shocked to hear anything any longer. He left the next day and subsequently *resigned* from the IAS. I don't know whether that little interaction I had with him that day had anything to do with his quitting the IAS.

Mr. Tyabji, however, called me the next day and gave me a dressing down in his beautiful stammering style.

"How dare you question what is happening?... You do not understand "Kashmiriyat" one bit... I will never invite you for any social gathering. Ever..."

Anyway, despite his supposedly deep understanding of "Kashmiriyat," Mr. Tyabji couldn't last long as Chief Secretary. In fact, he had to suffer the humiliation of serving as a mere Secretary of the Agriculture Department in the same Secretariat building which he had for a few months lorded over as Chief Secretary.

Restoring Normalcy and Falling Sick

MR. MURSHID before leaving had discussed with me how normalcy could be restored and I had suggested that it could start with the posting of direct recruit non-Kashmiri IAS officers as deputy commissioners in the valley. This could reduce the allegations of partisanship in the forthcoming elections leading to the ushering of a so-called "popular government" soon.

I was making this suggestion in the background of the infamous "Khalid DC," whose sole claim to fame was that he could *disqualify* the nomination papers of any non-National Conference candidate without batting an eyelid! That ensured uncontested victory for all Sheikh Abdullah nominees in the constituencies that Khalid DC was in-charge of.

Mr. Murshid jumped at the idea and posted officers like BR Sharma (IAS 1984) to Kupwara, BB Vyas (IAS 1986) to Srinagar, Sandip Nayak (IAS 1988) to Budgam and so on. This ultimately did result in the elections being held but there were stories galore of ballot boxes being stuffed by security personnel in favour of the National Conference. J&K could have its first free and fair elections only after the Electronic Voting Machines were introduced in 2002.

***

The horrors of being under a virtual house arrest in Srinagar got emphasised—when on one of my tours to Srinagar—I started experiencing extreme pain around my abdomen. I had some over-the-counter painkillers but I was vomiting continuously and my condition continued to deteriorate.

No doctor or hospital was available as no doctor was willing to treat an "outsider" or "Indian" in the existing government facilities. On DGP's orders, a Kashmiri doctor from the police hospital reported to me rather reluctantly. He gave me an injection for pain and tried to set up a saline drip for me. The doctor was so incompetent or flustered that he kept on pricking me but couldn't locate a vein for the drip. So, he left. And my hands had become like a red swollen balloon due to constant pricking.

The DG Police Mr. MN Sabbarwal heard of my plight and visited me in my room at Centaur. One look at my pale face and he took a decision to shift me to the army hospital before nightfall. He told me,

"Sonali, you may consider us incompetent or useless but our civil administration has totally collapsed. We can neither ensure your safety nor your treatment in any government hospital that we have. So, we have to go to the army hospital at Badami Bagh, NOW."

I was really reluctant to go to any army facility where I knew we lowly "civilians" generally have the last priority. But with the DGP and the DC Srinagar accompanying me I didn't have much to worry.

I had to undergo an emergency surgery the same night that lasted over *four hours*. And yes, the army's cussed rules didn't even allow my husband to spend the night in the hospital as my attendant. But I survived the ordeal and lived to tell the tale.

Chapter 13

Interacting with an "Outsider" Chief Secretary

IN 1994 NOVEMBER, Mr. Tyabji was replaced by Mr. Ashok Kumar (IAS 1965 JK) as Chief Secretary. The latter had seemed a nice person when he was coordinating with me in Delhi for those rare J&K IAS get-togethers while I served as Deputy Secretary in the Government of India. He was so unassuming that once when he wanted to convey his condolences on my father's demise, he used no official vehicle. Instead, he came on his personal scooter!

As soon as he joined as Chief Secretary, and when I formally called on him, his first question was, "Which department would you like to head?"

I said, "None, Sir... In fact, I was wanting to request you to send my name to Government of India."

And I explained my reasons as to how the J&K Government had already agreed to allow Arun, my husband, to go on deputation to Tata Energy Research Institute (TERI). On the request of Government of India where he was to head the Global Environmental Facility-United Nations Developmental Programme (GEF-UNDP) Himalayan Hilly Hydro project. Which he had himself written when he was Deputy Secretary in the Department of Non-Conventional Energy Sources.

Which was the first project to be approved from India by GEF with a grant (NOT loan) of US $ 15 million, and so on.

I also added how my child's education was suffering—as at that time—there were no good schools for boys in Jammu and the ones in Srinagar were totally out of bound for us "outsiders." My widowed mother living with me needed medical attention which was possible only in Delhi. I had also completed the Government of India's mandated two year serving period in J&K called the "cooling off." All in all, how essential was my going to Delhi.

The reaction of Mr. Ashok Kumar was extra-ordinary. He glared at me and said, "I hate people who want to go to Delhi."

That was strange coming from a person who had actually spent most of his career in Delhi, looking after his children's treatment or whatever!

Anyway, Mr. Ashok Kumar refused to send my name for central deputation. In fact, he hit back at Arun and before his orders for deputation to TERI were received, he transferred Arun from the post of Secretary Housing and Urban Development to the rather unimportant post of Joint Agrarian Reforms Commissioner.

Arun refused to join his "new assignment." Instead he pulled out his personal Maruti 800 and drove straight to Delhi to pursue his case personally. That took about a fortnight. With the order from the Central Department of Personnel sanctioning his deputation to TERI, an organisation "outside the Government" — he hired a private house in Delhi and came back to Jammu to pick us up.

My immediate boss was Mr. E.N. Murthy (IAS 1973), who was the Commissioner/Secretary Industries and Commerce. Being the lovely and understanding person he was, he allowed me to proceed on leave immediately.

Mr. Ashok Kumar didn't take kindly to this. He troubled Mr. Murthy so much, by *denying* him permission to visit his family in Delhi, etc. that he resigned from the IAS in 1995. I learnt later that Mr. Ashok Kumar's penchant for such "erratic behaviour" *perhaps* came from his indiscriminate use of anti-depressant drugs.

We didn't expect this level of hounding and unpleasantness from a supposedly honest "outsider" officer in J&K. *But when "outsiders" want to act more loyal than the king*, God help us all.

And all this was happening while the state was under Governor's rule supposedly being administered directly by the Central Government.

My "privilege leave" was getting over. Desperately, I had been requesting all and sundry to *please* forward my name to GOI for a posting. My heart leapt with joy when I learnt that *only my name had been forwarded.*

But what followed next totally *stumped* me.

Even while my name was being "circulated" to various Ministries by the Central Department of Personnel, Mr. Ashok Kumar got the Governor to write a letter to the then Prime Minister, Mr. Narasimha Rao (both Governor and the PM being from Andhra Pradesh shared a close bond) to the effect that no officer from J&K should be taken to the Government of India as that would impede the good General's efforts to "restore normalcy in J&K."

The PM marked the request to Secretary Department of Personnel & Trainings (DOPT) agreeing with the same. Since I was the only officer from J&K "on offer," this was all obviously *directed* at me. *No one cared to explain how I alone could restore normalcy in J&K.* But such was the level of personal animosity people stoop down to.

With the chances of my finding a posting in Delhi thus receding, I had no option but to apply for "study leave" that I was entitled to under All-India Services Rules. Since my husband was dealing with the Himalayan region and as I had some hands-on experience with J&K, I suggested that I be permitted to write a paper on the energy needs of women in the hilly areas and what could be done to make their quality of life better. The Governor's Secretary was Parvez Dewan (IAS 1977), who took pity on me, and somehow managed to get a one year study leave *sanctioned* despite Mr. Ashok Kumar, the Chief Secretary's, relentless objections.

Another year (1996) dawned and again I requested for my name to be sent to the Government of India. Surprisingly, by the middle of the year the J&K Government agreed to the idea. But postings in the Government of India take a while and so I had to request that my study leave be extended for another six months. This was within rules as IAS officers are entitled to two years of study leave during their service career, and I was asking for only one and a half years.

This time Mr. Ashok Kumar put his foot down and ordered that I report back to J&K right away.

"You can't keep on writing some *cooking recipes* in Delhi," he stated with a lot of disdain, and promptly got this "story" published in "The Daily Excelsior," a J&K newspaper on the front page!

Funnily, most of my Kashmiri friends who read that news were touched that I, an "outsider," was taking so much interest in cataloguing Kashmiri cuisine!

Meanwhile the stubborn streak in me had taken over, and I refused to return. In any case, I had no official accommodation to return to—as my lock on 18-A Government Quarters in Gandhinagar, Jammu was broken and the house forcibly taken over by another IAS officer, the moment I proceeded on the first phase of my earned leave of three months! This is J&K after all.

Immediately, my "leave salary" was stopped. *I felt my career in the IAS had come to an end.* Only darkness seemed to loom ahead. Thankfully, my husband was getting a salary. So, I didn't fortunately starve!

Well, every cloud has a silver lining. Soon elections were held in J&K (in 1996), and Dr. Farooq Abdullah was back in saddle. Farooq carried Mr. Ashok Jaitly (IAS 1964) with him from Delhi when he was going to Srinagar for his swearing in. At the airport itself, he announced that Mr. Jaitly would be the new Chief Secretary.

Mr. Ashok Kumar had to leave rather ignominiously. The horror he had unleashed on everyone especially us direct recruit "outsider" officers resulted in no one coming to even say goodbye to him. Unwept and unsung, this was his final departure from J&K cadre.

Proudly "Un-Empanelled" in Delhi

MY POSTING TO the Ministry of Human Resource Development (HRD), Department of Education had meanwhile come through. Mr. Jaitly ensured that I get my pending six months of pay (that Mr. Ashok Kumar had stopped) from the Resident Commissioner's Office in New Delhi without "reporting back" to J&K. He also "relieved" me to join my new duties in the Government of India by fax. There was no way I could thank him enough.

This time, however, New Delhi was not a *bed of roses*. Governments were being formed and falling in quick succession. Almost every few months, we were having a new Prime Minister. The negative impact that such an uncertainty had on the bureaucracy was there for all to see. Corruption and nepotism both reached a new zenith.

This was also the time that the great empanelment exercise for the post of Joint Secretary (JS) was to take place. Those were the days when no one used to tell you officially what *was* in your Annual Performance Reports (APRs) as these were all supposed to be "confidential." The smart ones *knew* what was written in their reports but *stupid* people like me (and my husband) were blissfully ignorant. Some of my IAS batch mates were surprised that we didn't even know the clerks in the Department of Personnel who were processing our case. Many were friends with them *offering* meals and gifts.

Soon the drama that is called "empanelment" started. Four Secretary level officers were supposed to go through all our APRs and then rank us. Most were too busy to do that themselves and so would leave it to their Private Secretaries "to do the needful." In case of one Secretary, one of our batch mates who was serving as her Director, was given the list. He happily came to his own conclusions as per his own *likes* and *dislikes* of his batch mates. All in all, this was the most arbitrary and non-transparent process of "selection" we had ever come across. We had no clue what was in our annual report, what we had been assessed for, and finally if we had made it to that coveted list or not.

It was only after my batch mates started getting posted as Joint Secretaries that I realised I had been *left out*. There was no way of knowing how or why.

The process was based solely on the kind of Annual Confidential Reports (ACRs) that we had. There were no interviews, no discussions, no attempt to find out why an officer had been judged adversely, and by whom...

For us placed in a corrupt, communal and anti-national cauldron that was J&K—it was a double whammy. If you joined hands with the local corrupt and anti-national elements, you would be everyone's favourite. But if you took a stand, your ACRs were "spoilt."

And because they were spoilt, you couldn't be empanelled in the Government of India. And if the latter happened, you had no *option* but to go back to stew in your cadre. Where willy-nilly you had to buy *peace* with the local politicians and try to survive. What a system the great Government of India had evolved!

We were thankful that the Union Public Service Commission (UPSC) didn't follow a similar process: of recruiting us in to the IAS solely on the basis of the reports that our class teachers had given us! With no reference to our marks in any written test or interviews or group interactions or extra-curriculars.

In my case, I realised that it was just not the communal and anti-national elements in J&K who had spoilt my ACRs but also some corrupt elements in the Government of India. For example, in the Department of Education—one of my assignments was to deal with the National Bal Bhavan. This was supposed to be an institution for promoting all-round development of children but had instead become a den of corruption. The lady ruling the roost was smart enough to extend privileges (like vehicles for the shopping of spouses, staff to help with domestic chores, etc.) to the Joint Secretary and even the Secretary.

Same was the situation in NCERT (National Council for Educational Research and Training) when I was given the additional charge of Secretary NCERT. On scrutiny, I found there was a *long* list of daily wagers, back door entrants into government service and people whose services were *not at all* required in the interest of NCERT. So, I *ordered* that we let them all go.

Immediately, I got a call from the Private Secretary to the then Secretary Education.

"Madam, the wife of the Secretary is very angry with you."

"But why?" I asked as I never had the privilege of meeting the lady.

"Because you have ordered that the services of her domestic help be dispensed with in the NCERT."

So, there went for a toss another of my ACRs. I realised that whenever I foolishly stepped in to trim any "wasteful" activity, the immediate impact was on my annual confidential report that these worthies had to write!

So, you have terrible reports in J&K and equally disastrous ones now in Delhi—God you must then be a terrible officer!

Fortunately, such bosses changed soon, and I again had a wonderful Joint Secretary Mr. Bhaskar Chatterjee and an extremely competent Secretary Ms. Achala Moulik to report to. My confidential reports were once again glowing and outstanding. But it was all a bit too late!

Anyway, my term at the Government of India came to an end by December 2001. Arun was already on deputation to ASSOCHAM (The Associated Chambers of Industry and Commerce in India) and finishing his Ph.D. in Energy Studies from IIT Delhi.

As my son was to complete his Class 12 board examinations soon, I requested Mr. Ashok Jaitly, the Chief Secretary, to let me be the OSD (officer on special duty) in the J&K House in Delhi which he very graciously allowed me to.

By May 2002, like *bad pennies*, we were back in J&K.

Chapter 14

Back to the Pavilion

MR. JAITLY, the Chief Secretary, was happy that I and Arun were returning to J&K, as scheduled, and asked me the department I would like to head. Since I was dealing with matters related to education in the Government of India and had been deeply associated with the formulation of the *Sarva Shiksha Abhiyaan* (Education for all) project, I suggested Education.

And Mr. Jaitly did just that. The last order he issued before retiring as Chief Secretary was to make me Commissioner/ Secretary of the Education Department.

This was the first time in my career when I had got a posting well in advance. I happily joined the day Secretariat opened in Srinagar after the bi-annual move. I was almost starry-eyed, wanting to implement the policies I had helped formulate in Delhi.

Meanwhile, Mr. Jaitly retired and Mr. I.S. Malhi (IAS 1966 JK) was made the Chief Secretary. Mr. Jaitly was retained by Dr. Farooq Abdullah as advisor but he no longer could take an active part in routine administrative decisions.

The year 2002 was important because, after six long years, elections were again due in J&K. In J&K, elections are held once in six years NOT in five as in the other states of the country.

Tackling the Mess that was Education

THE FIRST TASK that awaited me in my new assignment was to buy computers worth approximately four crores (forty million) for government colleges. Tenders had already been invited but with extremely funny specifications. No reputed firm with standard configurations/ specifications could thus participate. The idea was to favour the son-in-law of the-then Education Minister, who also happened to be the son of the Finance Minister. So I was briefed and had to be doubly careful.

The more I looked at the files, the more convinced I was that I couldn't go along with whatever my predecessor had done. So, I cancelled the tenders and made a 5-member committee comprising the HOD (Head of Department) of Computer Sciences of Jammu University and Kashmir University, a representative of DOEACC (A Government of India undertaking), the Director Colleges and the Financial Advisor of my department to frame and float fresh tenders.

My orders were duly carried out and the supply order was placed on one of the most reputed companies for branded computers in the country. The company was so thrilled that it agreed to place full-time an engineer at our disposal in J&K to ensure proper working of the installed computers. I also made the DOEACC validate each computer to ensure they met the specified standards. All in all, the process went through perfectly. The computers reached the colleges and were all made functional. No one raised a finger at this huge purchase.

But what I had to incur in the process was the *wrath* of Mr. Shafi Uri, the Education Minister. After I had ignored his *hints* to go as per his wishes, he prevailed upon Mr. Malhi, the Chief Secretary, to *split* the Department of Education that I was heading. So, the school education portion was spliced away and given to a very junior promoted officer while I was left with the higher and technical education parts, ONLY.

The Education Minister couldn't transfer me because he was not sure the Chief Minister would agree. Mr. Malhi was happy to connive because he thought I was a favourite of Mr. Jaitly, who he was extremely jealous of. Mr. Malhi had come to the IAS from the ex-servicemen quota, which meant that he had to appear in even lesser number of papers (eight in those days) than all other category of IAS officers. For that "favour," he always was a little less sure of his abilities and wanted to compensate by currying favours with the politicians.

I had returned to the cadre after nearly eight years and so had to accept this change without a murmur. When I met Mr. Jaitly at an official dinner, he expressed his *unhappiness* at what had happened. He, however, added that since I had been away for a *long time*, probably people had *forgotten* what an excellent officer I was.

"Okay, sir, this time I will stay and work and make sure nobody forgets me," I assured him.

Getting in the Cross-Hairs of Mr. Malhi

MEANWHILE, THE CLASS 12 results were announced, and it was college time for my son who wanted to have a liberal arts education. So, time to apply to various colleges in Delhi University. Thankfully, his marks were good, and he made it to both Venkateshwar and Hindu College. For his admission, I had to go to Delhi and since all my friends were still in the Ministry for Human Resource Development (HRD), they did oblige me by inviting me for some important meetings.

But after we reached Delhi, I realised that besides "cut-offs," St. Stephen's College, which also my son had applied to, conducts interviews and that too after all the admission process for all other colleges was over. I, therefore, applied for two days of casual leave, paid the fees at Venkateshwara College to reserve my son's seat there and then let my son attend his interviews at St. Stephen's. As luck would have it, my son not only got admission in St. Stephen's College but also got hostel accommodation within the college premises.

This was one big headache off. We all returned happily to Srinagar only to face unbelievable *hostility*. Why? Because my son had got admission in a college which, as Mr. Malhi told me himself, both he and his son could only *admire* from outside its gates!

Middle of July came, and I needed to go to Delhi to settle down my son in the hostel. I had myself studied in the Lady Shri Ram (LSR) and Miranda House in Delhi University and so knew the little knick-knacks like buckets, mugs, foldable mattress (the rooms had to be vacated during summer vacations), etc. that were required by every hosteller. This time I requested Secretary, Ministry of Culture, who was a friend and he asked me to meet him to discuss some funding for J&K.

Mr. Malhi, however, *refused* me permission to go for the meeting. When I asked him why, he replied that it was because I had taken two days of casual leave the last time I had gone on official duty! I tried to explain my compulsions but to no avail. I therefore *cancelled* my meeting and instead applied for leave. St. Stephen's had affected Malhi so deeply that even this was *denied*. I then applied for medical leave and proceeded without waiting for his sanction.

These were the peculiar circumstances one was working in. But after this "defiance," Mr. Malhi simply refused to let me attend any meeting in Delhi no matter how important it was for J&K, lest I meet my son in Delhi!

Strangely though whenever a detailed note was required for the education sector, Mr. Malhi expected me to give one for the entire sector whereas I was dealing with only the higher and the technical education part. One day he *screamed* at me and asked me whether I was even capable of giving him such a complete/comprehensive report or not.

I told him I could give him one for the entire government including sectors like PWD, Health, etc. but my responsibilities were restricted to higher and technical education currently and, therefore, it would be inappropriate if I started meddling in the affairs of other departments.

I knew in government, sometimes an officer is nominated to co-ordinate with other departments to help prepare a joint note or project report. But that would have required the issue of a proper order empowering the "co-ordinator" to co-ordinate with offices which are not normally under her control. But that would have also meant giving credit to me for such co-ordinating efforts which Mr. Malhi wanted to avoid. I can only imagine how angry "my defiance" must have then made him.

Arrival of Mr. Mufti Mohammad Sayeed

ANY WAY THE state elections were soon upon us. The pariahs we *outsiders* are, we were, of course, *not allowed* to vote. Even now, it surprises many Indians, including many of our rather knowledgeable batch mates that in J&K all outsider/non-state subject officers are *dis-enfranchised* 100%. That may be totally against the *fundamental rights* given to us under the Indian Constitution, but who cares?

The election results threw up quite a surprise. Against all intelligence reports, Omar Abdullah lost from Ganderbal, which has been an old borough of the Abdullahs. His party National Conference lost its majority. Mr. Shafi Uri too lost badly and could never regain his seat till I remained in service.

A new political combination of the People's Democratic Party (PDP) and the Congress was taking shape. Mr. G.C. Saxena, the Governor, wanted the outgoing Chief Minister Dr. Farooq Abdullah to continue as a caretaker CM, but Farooq refused hoping to put pressure on the Congress party to align with him. That gambit, however, didn't succeed and a new government headed by Mufti Mohammad Sayeed was sworn in on the second of November 2002.

The Secretariat had already closed for its bi-annual move to Jammu. We were in Delhi during the "move days." But our sojourn was cut short as Arun had to rush back to Srinagar, to a vacant house (as all our luggage had already gone to Jammu), to make arrangements for the swearing-in ceremony in the Sher-i-Kashmir International Convention Centre (SKICC).

It was the first such function that Arun had to conduct himself acting as the lead announcer and every one praised him for the way he handled that. I watched the swearing-in function in Srinagar from Jammu on TV and enjoyed watching my husband playing a major role in the whole process.

Mr. Malhi retired after a month's extension but kept on waiting in Jammu hoping for some post-retirement assignments which never came. His lobbying for making him the Vice Chancellor of the Agricultural University was shot down by the Governor Mr. G.C. Saxena (who Arun was then Secretary of) on the grounds that Malhi was not even a Ph.D.

I don't know why Mr. Malhi couldn't believe that for a rank "outsider" like him such favours are NOT showered in routine in J&K.

For that, your *bootlicking* abilities have to be of an exceptional order, I suppose, and apparently, Mr. Malhi failed on that account.

Chapter 15

Only Pliable "Locals" Allowed as Chief Secretary

THE NEW COMBINATION of PDP and Congress that had emerged after the state elections decided to have Mufti Mohammed Sayeed of the PDP as Chief Minister (CM) and Mangat Ram Sharma of the Congress as Deputy CM. Some members of the Panthers Party—a Jammu based party were also included in the cabinet to provide the much-needed stability to the government.

The new government brought in Mr. Sudhir Bloeria, who belonged to Jammu, as Chief Secretary, after superseding quite a few "outsider" officers of the 1967 and 1968 batches. Mufti was hell-bent on establishing the principle of having only local officers as Chief Secretary regardless of the havoc it would cause on the morale of the "outsider" officers who could also be more competent.

Mr. Bloeria was an ex-serviceman and had got into the IAS in 1972. Like Malhi, he too didn't take the prescribed eight papers that all others, including the reserved category candidates, had to take. Still, as per rules in those days, he was awarded a 4-year benefit in seniority. So, while he trained with the 1972 batch officers, he had on paper the seniority of 1968. That created a piquant situation for all 1972 batch officers who till the other day had "Sudhired" him and now had to "Sir" him as he was now the Chief Secretary.

Making a *Jammu-wala* Chief Secretary was a clever move by Mufti to help carry forward his Kashmir centric *anti-national* agenda. He had earlier appointed Iqbal Khandey (IAS 1978) as his Principal Secretary. Iqbal was the second Kashmiri Muslim direct recruit in the IAS.

We knew Iqbal from our days in Baramulla and had attended his wedding there. He was married to Kaneez, the eldest daughter of Mr. Shams-ud-Din, who was the DC in Baramulla.

Later we learnt that Iqbal was adopted in his childhood by Mr. Shams-ud-Din. All his expenses on schooling, college education etc. were then paid for by Shams Sahib with the understanding that Iqbal will be his *Khana-damaad,* or a son-in-law who stays with his father-in-law after marriage.

Apparently, this was a very common practice in Kashmir for folks who had no sons. Strangely, *Sharia* (the Islamic Laws) doesn't recognise this practice of adoption but Kashmiris in those days couldn't care less.

Iqbal was originally allotted to Tamil Nadu, from where his cadre was changed to J&K in "public interest," after a forceful intervention from Sheikh Abdullah.

Being a Kashmiri, Iqbal just couldn't adjust in Madurai (Tamilnadu) to the practice of having *sambhar* (a spicy lentil *daal* dish) served three-times-a-day with all his meals. His views on the use of coconut oil for cooking mirrored mine. But what troubled Iqbal most was the strict prohibition in force in Tamilnadu and he told us the lengths he had to go, to get his daily booze on "medical grounds!"

Interestingly, Mr. Mohammad Shafi Pandit (IAS 1969), the first direct recruit Kashmiri Muslim IAS officer, was not allowed to become Chief Secretary because Iqbal knew that it would have then diluted his own position. Instead having a *pliant* Chief Secretary from Jammu suited Iqbal much more.

So poor Mr. M.S. Pandit. A brilliant officer otherwise, he had to be shunted out as Chairman of the J&K Public Service Commission, even before his retirement, to make way for Mr.

Bloeria. *And J&K in the process lost out a historic opportunity to make its first direct recruit Kashmiri Muslim IAS officer its Chief Secretary.*

Interestingly, Iqbal used to "Sir" Mr. M.S. Pandit but NOT Mr. Bloeria, who was technically one year senior to Mr. Pandit and 10 years senior to Iqbal! That was, however, quite a small price that Mr. Bloeria had to pay for getting the top position in J&K.

I may mention here that Iqbal also used to claim to be one of the founders of the PDP as he had an adversarial relationship with Farooq Abdullah. Both used to be quite thick earlier but when Farooq came back to power in 1996 they "broke up," for reasons that are mentioned only in hushed tones.

Moving to Industries

WITH THE NEW government in saddle, some changes in the administrative set up were inevitable. To my surprise, I found the higher and technical education split up further and I was now left with only the technical education part!

Fate intervened, and I had to proceed on leave for a month for undergoing a major abdominal surgery arising out of the complications connected with the earlier surgery at the Army Hospital in Srinagar. As soon as I joined back, I was transferred and given the Industries and the Commerce Department.

I couldn't believe my good fortune. As I have mentioned, the handloom and handicraft sectors, which were part of the Industries set up in J&K, were really close to my heart. Also willy-nilly, I had acquired a lot of hands-on experience in these sectors. I thought I could now go all-out to help the state economy by harnessing the full potential of this sector.

Mr. Atal Bihari Vajpayee was the Prime Minister (PM). He visited Srinagar in April 2003 and I helped organise one of his meetings with local industrialists. The PM was keen that more self-employment generation programmes be initiated as there was too much dependence on government for providing jobs.

He also announced a special package for J&K for which we had to now formulate special projects.

I went about my job rather seriously and made a proposal for setting up a central Craft Development Institute and an Institute of Carpet Technology, which were both approved. Then I formulated a detailed industrial policy for J&K, which incidentally continued till 2016, when it was supposed to be valid only for five years!

To improve the design and the productivity of the craftspeople, I helped organise as many as seventeen designer workshops in Srinagar. The best designers of the country participated. The National Institute of Fashion Technology was roped in to have a fashion show using textiles and embroideries of J&K.

The enthusiasm in the craftspeople was unparalleled. There was a concern amongst older craftsmen that their children were not joining their family business because it was not remunerative enough. My initiatives gave them hope that finally their hard work would bear fruit and they could all have both recognition and means for a decent living.

In the organised industry sector, I had some of the biggest names in the country like LG, Samsung, Berger Paints, lining up for permissions. The ease of doing business in J&K was being talked of everywhere. I remember a company head telling me that he had not come across such smiling and helpful faces in the industry department anywhere else in the whole country.

Industries was a huge department with as many as fourteen heads of department and managing directors (MDs) of public sectors undertakings reporting to me. But there was complete harmony everywhere. I remember Salim Beg, my Director Industries, telling me that working now was giving him great joy. Also, that if the government could give me a five-year tenure, J&K would become a truly developed state.

But I was already stepping on so many *toes*. Mr. Mangat Ram Sharma, the Deputy Chief Minister, was my minister. He had six sons who were not doing anything much. So, he "allotted" them different heads of department (HODs) and PSUs to "deal with." The problem was that whenever they approached any HODs and MDs for any favours, they would invariably tell them that whatever work they wanted done had to come through me, the Commissioner Secretary.

Now, I suppose, because of my frank and no nonsense reputation, none of the sons dared approach me. But that was just the lull before the storm.

Just after 5 months, Mr. Mangat Ram Sharma hit back, and I was *transferred*. And not me alone. As many as 73 persons in the industries and commerce were transferred along with me. That included all HODs, all managing directors and officers even up to the district level.

Why? Because they were all apparently "my men." But they had all been working in the department before me and were in any case all locals. So how did they become my men? But that was it.

The people who came and wept in my room were the craftsmen. "Madam, you showed us such a beautiful dream and now you're abandoning us before we have reached the shore." My heart wept with them but what could I do? I was like a bonded labour doing only what my masters wanted me to do.

Another interesting fact about my transfer was that I was not being replaced by another serving IAS officer. Instead, Mr. A. Sahasranaman, a retired IAS officer from Tamil Nadu, who had taken voluntary retirement a good ten years back was brought on contract as Principal Secretary Industries and Commerce. True, he had once belonged to the 1973 batch of the IAS in J&K, but can a person who *quit* ten years back, be brought back on a *regular* "IAS cadre post?"

Yes, *retired* IAS officers do become advisors, governors, politicians or even ministers. But a regular Secretary to Government? That was unheard of. So why this unusual favour?

We learnt that first, he was friendly with Mr. Mufti Sayeed's daughter who lived in Chennai. But the second, and the more *important* reason was that before he became Chief Secretary, Mr. Bloeria had a mild heart attack on a visit to Chennai and Mr. Sahasranaman had helped him get suitable treatment. That was a debt that Mr. Bloeria had to repay. *Largesse* and *nepotism* is something J&K in any case thrives on.

Interestingly, Mr. Sahasranaman who was only a Commissioner Secretary when he took voluntary retirement, was "promoted" as Principal Secretary, while he spent 10 years in retirement! And now he was brought back with none of the baggage of the IAS like conduct rules, appraisal reports, etc. that we *lowlifes* were saddled with. How wonderful!

I was the Secretary of the IAS Association and we decided to protest. In fact, I knew the President of the Central IAS association and *asked* him whether such actions were *permissible.* And his answer was a categorical NO. In fact, he spoke to Mr. Bloeria, and this *angered* the Chief Secretary even more.

We went in a deputation to Mr. Bloeria and requested him that if he really wanted to help Mr. Sahasranaman, he could make him an Officer on Special Duty (OSD), or Advisor, with the rank of a Minister of State but putting him on a cadre post of "Secretary to Government" was a different matter. Mr. Bloeria was wild.

He shouted that I was protesting *only* because I had been transferred. So instead of addressing the issue, the attack was turned on me and personalised. Obviously, that was the end of the matter. Mr. Bloeria also took upon himself to give me a nasty appraisal that finished of my chances of escaping to the Government of India forever.

General Sinha Arrives

MEANWHILE ANOTHER change took place in J&K. Mr. Girish Chandra Saxena had completed his five-year term and in his place Lt. General (Retd.) S.K. Sinha was appointed as the

Governor of J&K. Our earlier experience with General Krishna Rao had really prejudiced us about the functioning of Army officers in a civilian setting. As Arun was then the Secretary to the Governor, he would have been directly in the *firing* line. Maybe it was now time for him to get a change but there was no one willing to come to replace him in the Raj Bhavan.

Meanwhile General Sinha, who was then the Governor of Assam, called Arun to Delhi for a briefing at the end of which both took an instant liking for each other. Rest is, of course, history.

A very interesting incident took place in my life during this period. Long back, even before my son was born, I had gone to Pahalgam and then to Chandanwari to see the glacier over River Lidder. Someone told me that this was the traditional route to the Holy Cave shrine of Amarnath. The desire to go to Amarnath overwhelmed me but—a look at the high mountains—and I had to very reluctantly abandon the idea. Instead I prayed, "God please do give me *darshan* (audience) when my son becomes 18, and please let me come on a helicopter."

General Sinha took over as Governor in J&K in June 2003. As Governor, he was also the Chairman of the Vaishno Devi as well Amarnath Shrine Board. For the latter, the auspicious month of the pilgrimage had dawned and the Governor and his wife decided to go for *darshans* on the first day.

Although Arun was till then the CEO of only the Vaishno Devi Shrine Board (and NOT the Amarnath Shrine Board), General Sinha still asked Arun to accompany him. Then on a whim, and because there was still some space left in the state helicopter that was taking them to the shrine, he asked him to bring his wife and son along.

As I sat in the chopper at Nehru Helipad waiting to take off, I suddenly realised that Baba Amarnath was granting me a wish made so many years back. My son had turned 18, and I was going by chopper. This was the first *darshan* of my life that

I had of the 14 ft. high naturally occurring ice lingam and what an experience it was.

On return Arun was also given the charge of CEO, Amarnath Shrine Board. Baba Amarnath seemed to have really blessed us. But this was J&K and more was to follow.

Chapter 16

Back to Education

AFTER FIVE HECTIC months in the super-active Industries Department, I was back to the rather *sedate* but familiar surroundings of the Higher Education Department. Surprisingly, this time I had the additional charge of Technical Education, Youth Services and Sports and even Culture, Archives and Museums. The welcome I received from the staff of the various institutions was unbelievable. Even officers in the Ministry of Human Resource Development in the Government of Indian (MHRD) were thrilled to have me back.

The processes I had started in my last *avatar* in this department could now be carried forward. To improve the morale of my teachers, I ordered—on priority—completion of the promotion process of principals. This was done and soon my colleges had well-motivated and qualified persons heading them. In addition, I initiated the process of national accreditation for both the Jammu as well as the Kashmir University and also for the various colleges.

In parallel, we made an assessment of the number of colleges we needed to cater to the growing number of students seeking higher education. We worked out that if we had 14 new colleges with full facilities, this could take care of the demand in J&K for the next 50 years.

I made a detailed report and took it to the Government of India for funding. So far, setting up of new colleges had never been funded by the Government of India; so, they asked me to approach the University Grants Commission (UGC) which is the organisation dealing with higher education at the national level.

I met and cajoled and convinced all my contacts in the Ministry and the UGC, and finally the project was approved. This had NEVER happened in J&K. My Minister Mr. Harsh Dev Singh who was from the Panthers Party was so *thrilled* that he came down to my room to congratulate me.

Next, I personally visited all the colleges and technical institutions all over Kashmir, including in Sopore, which is supposedly a den of militancy. To my surprise, the students welcomed me with the song *"Sare Jahan Se Achcha Hindustan Hamara."*

When a politician heard of the incident, he asked sarcastically. "What are you trying to do? Make them all Indians?"

"But aren't they already?" I retorted.

The politician, I'm sure, would have muttered under his breath,

"How stupid could this *'outsider'* be?"

Sure, there was enough *anti-nationalism* in the education sector. But in my experience, it was more prevalent among the *pampered* faculty of the Kashmir University than in government colleges and schools. That was obviously because the university bigwigs were *getting funds* from across the *border*.

Any way I still motivated the Kashmir University to apply for national accreditation and they did feel proud when they managed an "A" grade.

Improving ITIs

ANOTHER ISSUE which was troubling me was the quality of education and the employability of the students being churned out of our colleges. We worked out a formula of introducing optional vocational courses with one-year certificate courses, two-year diploma courses, and three-year advance diploma courses which could be pursued along with the normal BA/ BSc degrees.

The results were amazing. I met 30 boys and girls doing advance diploma courses in mass communication in the Baramulla College. Each one of them had a job even before they had graduated. The best had a job with a local TV station, or with local newspapers, and the weakest with a video maker for marriages.

In the technical education sector, the ITIs (Industrial Training Institutes) which provided basic human resource training were quite an ignored lot. I managed to make a sub-package for them out of the Prime Minister's overall industrial package, which I had got approved in my earlier assignment, to help upgrade them.

Initially, there was a lot of resistance from various ministries, but I argued that with the coming of new industrial units in J&K, there would be a need for skilled workers. Also, if we did not train workers in J&K, they would simply come from outside the state, thus defeating the very purpose of setting up these industries.

The PMO liked my logic and finally prevailed upon the concerned ministries to approve my up-gradation proposal along with some new courses.

Revitalizing Archives and Museums

THE MOST IGNORED department under my charge was the one dealing with Archives and the Museums. The directors, though all Muslims from Kashmir, seemed to be quite a *hated* lot. Why, I just couldn't understand. When I tried to dig deeper, my discovery *shocked* me.

They were hated because they were focussing on the "pre-Islamic" period in Kashmir which is a *taboo* as per the instructions from across the border. Most of the carvings and sculptures that were there in our museums were related to the Shaivite and the Buddhist periods. The Pakistani logic is that if these periods of history are NOT kept away from public memory, the public may get enamoured with their heritage and even abandon Islam!

A very interesting incident took place during this time. The famous Pakistani troupe "Ajoka" from Lahore came to Jammu University and performed the play "Bulleh Shah" in Punjabi. Now, Dogri, the language spoken in Jammu is very close to Punjabi and, therefore, the audience had no problem understanding the play.

Enthused, the Pakistani troupe expressed a desire to perform in Srinagar. Now most *Kashmiris* can't understand a *single word* of Punjabi, and so I suggested that they would need to add some explanations in Urdu to enable Kashmiris to appreciate the play. The look of horror and surprise on their faces was amazing.

"What? Kashmiris don't speak Punjabi?"

So much for the Pakistani claim over Kashmir. *And so much for the ignorance of Kashmiris who want to be a part of Pakistan!*

Focusing on the Universities

WHILE I WAS busy polishing up the higher and technical education sector, my husband was involved in setting up the SMVDU (Shri Mata Vaishno Devi University). So far, except for our stints in Udhampur and Leh, our paths had not officially crossed. But since the Governor was also the chancellor of all universities in J&K, I was now officially interacting with my colleague who was also my husband.

Since we were the only IAS couple in the cadre so far, some people felt *uncomfortable* at our working together. Especially on a project which by name (Vaishno Devi) didn't sound *secular*. But we couldn't care less and went out of our comfort zones to turn SMVDU in to the best engineering and management institution in J&K.

Arun, of course, was also busy professionalising the

functioning of those two world famous Shrine Boards viz. Shri Mata Vaishno Devi Shrine Board (SMVDSB) and Shri Amarnathji Shrine Board (SASB) in so many other spheres. As Chief Executive Officer of both these shrines for over six years from May 2002 to June 2008, he was singularly responsible for introducing a helicopter service that was run with private sector efficiency but with public sector transparency in fixing fares. He went out of his way to make pilgrimage especially for the old and the infirm accessible (and affordable) by introducing pollution-free battery-operated buses. Mobile telephony, digital display of group numbers on plasma screens to reduce waiting in queues, on-line facilities for issuing pilgrimage slips, receiving donations, reserving rooms and securing helicopter bookings, free enclosed steel lockers that reduced the complaints of thefts considerably, wide train-style bunk beds that at one go doubled the dormitory capacities, a 700-bedded dormitory accommodation called *Trikuta Bhavan* that is held by many to be the best *dharmashala* in India, a new water supply scheme, a sewage treatment plant, finding NGOs to run dispensaries and free eateries (langars).... Almost every new step in these two shrines was conceived, progressed and accomplished during Arun's tenure.

And then January 2004 arrived with us completing 25 years in the IAS. We were to now get the Principal Secretary's grade and were apprehensive of the fight in store for us in getting this promotion.

To our surprise, this was one promotion we were given with no effort. This was the *penultimate* grade in the IAS scheme of things with just one more promotion to wait for. The headlines in the newspapers screamed, "Double promotions to the Kumars!"

After a long time, I was comfortable in my assignment. I had two cabinet ministers—one from the Panthers' Party and another from Kargil—who were both extremely nice. My fame as an able administrator was growing by leaps and bounds. But could this be allowed to continue? Could the minds of the youth be changed from anti-Indian activities to something more positive? Could I possibly be allowed to continue? The answer once again was a deafening NO.

One of my last acts as Principal Secretary Higher Education was to get Rupees 20 crores (200 million) for the Jammu University. The Prime Minister, Mr. Vajpayee had announced a grant of Rupees 30 crores (300 million) and the Vice Chancellor Prof. Amitabh Mattoo was thrilled about it. When I asked him whether he had actually received the money, he *was stunned*. I told him that such announcements are routine in the Government of India, and they have to be "followed up" to reach any logical conclusion.

So together we went to the MHRD (Ministry of Human Resources Development). The Joint Secretary Ravi Mathur was my batch mate, and I asked him to help. He was a little sceptical about the "capacity" of the Jammu University to utilise such a huge sum. I tried my best to convince him. I told him that elections were due end of 2004 and who knows who will be the next PM. But poor Jammu University would be deprived of this grant if Ravi delayed the release of funds.

Ravi finally relented and sanctioned Rupees 20 crores (200 million). That was all that the Jammu University got out of the PM's package—not a penny more. Today the Zorawar auditorium that was built with this money stands a testimony to this effort.

Chapter 17

Moving to Forest

THIS TIME MY ouster from Education was achieved in a unique fashion. Mr. Bloeria, the Chief Secretary, knew—that since both my cabinet ministers were ecstatic with my performance, they would not agree to my transfer. So, he cleverly made out a case—that since the Forest Department is an extremely important department that also deals with an All-India Service viz. the Indian Forest Service—it must be headed by a Principal Secretary rank IAS officer.

Sounds logical, notwithstanding that this poor All-India Service in J&K was till then left at the mercy of local officers who could be even *twenty years* junior to the Principal Chief Conservator of Forests who heads this service in every state.

But the real reason was that my tenure in the education sector had to be cut short and for this—it was easier that I be "kicked up."

This concept of a department being more important or less important in the government has always eluded me. In Government of India, it used to be the number of *foreign trips* you could manage. This was because such trips entitled you to extra tax-free money in the shape of DSAs (Daily Subsistence Allowances) that you could save by skimping on your meals.

Another criterion of your department's importance was the number of Public Sector Undertakings (PSUs) you controlled. That ensured that you always had an extra-vehicle or two for your spouse and children and a room in five star hotels when you went on tours—all at the expense of that poor PSU.

At the state level, the sole criterion was the *number of persons* you could transfer. Because each transferee had to pay some *speed-money* to get a posting of his/her choice. So, if you charged, say Rupees 20,000 on an average, for transferring a teacher to a capital city like Jammu or Srinagar, and you took out a list of 50 such transfers, you could earn 20,000*50= Rupees 10 lakhs (a million)! And you could do this every 3 months sharing part of the booty with your bosses and keep everyone happy. No wonder, the only industry that can still thrive in J&K is the "transfer industry!"

The other source of "earning" was the commission you could earn on getting construction projects executed through contractors. This was more prevalent in the engineering departments (like Roads and Buildings, Power Development, Irrigation or Public Health Engineering), where no one needed to break in to a sweat for getting the routine 10% "commission."

On both these criteria, education was more "important" than forest, and so I had to be shifted out. Anyway, I couldn't care less and happily moved as Principal Secretary Forest.

Rescuing the Indian Forest Service (IFoS)

THE FIRST THING which struck me in the new department was the extremely *wonky* cadre management. There were litigations galore. As in IAS and IPS, there was a parallel cadre of non-IFoS officers holding posts meant *only* for the IFoS officers. Promotions of local officers to the IFoS had been delayed *abnormally*. The result, while the direct recruits were reduced to *tears*, the local officers had become *sullen* and frustrated.

I realised that the IFoS was the first All-India Service which was degraded and almost *destroyed* to aid Pak-backed terrorism in J&K. The state's forest wealth was so immense that in Maharaja's time, the richest persons in the state used to be the forest lessees. To loot this wealth, the regular forest service had to be destroyed first.

And to do that, first "outsider" IFoS officers had to be moved *out* of the crucial posts of District Forest Officers (DFOs). Then local officers, *without* being promoted to the IFoS, were *allowed* to take over these posts. This allowed the *plundering* of the forest wealth of J&K on a scale that was unheard of.

Surprisingly, even local officers didn't like this "system" much. Because with no "system," they too could then be replaced by any other Tom, Dick or Harry—anyone willing to do his master's bidding with no questions asked.

With great difficulty and despite a lot of resistance from various quarters, I first pushed through a thorough "cadre review" of the IFoS posts in J&K. This meant *cataloguing* which posts could be held by only IFoS officers (local or outsider, promoted or direct recruits) and which could not.

This needed some kind of reconciliation between the local promoted officers and direct recruits. The futility of instituting court cases against each other was staring everyone in the face and we all agreed to sort out the matters in-house. Thankfully, we succeeded and today the Forest Service has become one of the better managed service in the state, I hope!

And the Endangered Species

IN THIS ASSIGNMENT, I found that if the Kashmir politicians *hated* one department, it was the one dealing with wild life preservation. During the time of the Maharaja, it used to be called the Department of Games and Fisheries. And it existed only to issue permits for shooting wild animals and for angling.

It was as late as in 1978 that a Wildlife Preservation Act was passed in J&K. But the attitude towards the wild life still remained the same. I would often read in newspapers the exploits of "shikaris" like Dr. Farooq Abdullah who would *shoot* hundreds of migratory birds in a single day!

In fact, I remember, an obnoxious minister asking me why I always seemed to speak on behalf of bears and leopards, who were a "threat" to Kashmiris.

"Because sir, bears and leopards do not know how to speak your language and vote in your constituency. That's why Government of India has put crazy officers like me to look after their interests."

I said that with a smile in as *light-hearted* a manner as possible, but the repartee *infuriated* the minister no end.

As elsewhere, growing human habitations were *infringing* on wild life areas and once in a while there would be a stray incident of someone getting mauled by a bear or a leopard. Sadly, when the wild life staff would arrive on the scene, they would be greeted with stones and the slogans which would be the usual *"Hum kya chahe azadi (we want freedom) .... Jeeve jeeve Pakistan (Hope Pakistan lives)!"*

I don't think the villagers believed that if they had joined the Islamic State of Pakistan, they could kill all wild animals with impunity and live happily ever after. But they would still chant such *nonsensical* slogans because they can't think of chanting any other slogan in Kashmir that requires some *thinking* on their part.

And the Forests and the Lakes

ENCROACHMENT ON forest land, uncontrolled felling of trees, filling up of water bodies—all were matters of serious concern. In my attempt to find solutions, I came across some very *interesting* facts. As a probationer in Baramulla, I had been awed by the beauty of the biggest fresh water lake of Asia—the Wular lake. Suddenly, it had all but *disappeared*. And it was the Forest Department which seemed to have played a *major* role in that. Shocking but true!

To meet the firewood needs of Srinagar and adjoining areas, they had planted hundreds of thousands of trees, especially willow, in and around the lake. The willow sucked up all the water and soon paddy fields had moved inside the lake. Of course, all this was done at the instance and instigation of politicians in connivance with local untrained and ill-qualified forest staff who didn't know any better. This is the price we had to pay for ignoring professionals; and unfortunately, it was the same story in every other department.

Funnily, all this was financed by the Government of India, through their "social forestry" projects. And so, they were equal partners in this massive ecological disaster that was taking place right in front of our eyes!

On the other hand, there was a *reluctance* of some forest officials to give *clearance* for projects of national importance like highways and railways.

Under the social forestry programme, trees had been planted on both sides of the national highway. When the highways had to be widened, some trees had to be cut. However, some senior forest officers held up the cutting by claiming that wherever more than five trees existed, the area became a "forest" which could not be "removed" without following the usually cumbersome environmental clearance procedures.

"But doesn't this defeat the very purpose of social forestry?" I asked, "Especially when you do have another scheme for compensatory forest afforestation."

Anyway, we did overcome such resistance and were moving on when something very dramatic happened.

The Amarnath Land Issue

THE YATRA (PILGRIMAGE) to the Holy Shrine of Lord Amarnath in South Kashmir, which finds mention in so many holy scriptures of Hindus, had been going on for hundreds of years. In the rainy season of Shravan (June-July) every year, pilgrims used to trudge for three-four days in high altitude areas to reach a massive 80 ft. high cave and to admire a stunning 14 ft. high ice *Shiv Lingam* that is formed naturally.

With Kashmir overrun by Muslim invaders, the route to this pilgrimage was forgotten for some 300 years. Till a Muslim shepherd called Buta Malik, whose family is still associated with this yatra, stumbled upon the cave and reported his discovery to his Hindu friends who re-started the pilgrimage.

The yatra is so arduous that even today 3-4 pilgrims die on an average, EVERY DAY, *mostly* on account of cardiac failures. In 1996, when J&K was under Governor's Rule, thousands got stuck in a snow blizzard on this route and over 300 people were killed. The survivors were totally miserable with no food and water for days.

An enquiry conducted by Mr. Nitish Sen Gupta, a senior IAS officer, castigated the State Government for total mismanagement and suggested that a shrine board, similar in nature to the already successful Shri Mata Vaishno Devi Shrine Board (SMVDSB), be set up by the State Government. This board could then regulate the numbers of pilgrims allowed on this route and also make the required arrangements for them.

Acting on these recommendations, the Farooq Abdullah Government set up the Shri Amarnath Shrine Board (SASB) with an initial grant of Rupees One crore (10 million). This board too like SMVDSB was headed by the Governor, but there was one very important difference. Whereas over 100,000 kanals (12,500 acres) of land, including forest land, was transferred to the Shri Mata Vaishno Devi Shrine Board (SMVDSB) by Mr. Jagmohan through an Ordinance in 1986, the SASB Act *didn't* transfer even an inch of any state or forest land to SASB.

However, the Amarnath Shrine Board was still expected to provide all facilities to the pilgrims at its cost, which was hitherto the responsibility of the State Government. This included the setting up of temporary shelters, toilets, hospitals, eateries (langars), etc.

State Government would still look after security and provide staff on deputation for temporary duties but that was all. The flak for any deaths or disaster had to be now taken by the SASB. This was all going on all right till Mr. Mufti Sayeed became the Chief Minister in 2002.

Mufti felt that if this yatra to Baba Amarnath became as popular as the one to Mata Vaishno Devi in Jammu region, it would "dilute the Muslim-majority character" of Kashmir and constitute a "cultural invasion." This was in any case the *dominant thought* among the communal and anti-national elements in Kashmir but what was *disturbing* was—that Mufti was pandering to this thought so unabashedly.

The Sufi-syncretic culture of Kashmir was already dead with the exodus of Kashmiri Pandits in the 1990s. I found it hard to believe when a prominent Muslim minister of Mufti's cabinet showed Arun the *Rudraksh* chain (that only Hindus sport) he used to wear secretly under his shirt and *admitted* with some nostalgia that he was taught the *Holy Quran* by Kashmiri Pandit teachers in school.

Anyway, the short point is that Mufti soon set out to create as many *hurdles* as possible in the path of the SASB as he could.

With Mr. Saxena on his way out, no one protested much in 2003. But by 2004, a new Governor (Gen. SK Sinha) and a new CEO (Arun) were firmly in the saddle. There was yet another complication.

As per the Hindu calendar, this was a "malmas," meaning there would be two *Shravans* in 2004. This happened because like most ancient calendars, Hindu lunar months have just 28 days. That means that every year they are short by 29-30 days as compared to the 365-366-day English calendar. This they compensate by having an extra month every year. And to Mufti's chagrin, in 2004, this meant having an additional rainy month of Shravan.

Now since the pilgrimage to all Shiva shrines in India, including Amarnath, is held in the month of *Shravan*, in 2004 it had to be now spread *over two months*. But Mufti would have nothing of that.

That led to a huge showdown. With Mufti and all communal elements of Kashmir on one side and the Hindu priests on the other. The *pseudo-environmentalists* also joined in with a chorus about how Hindu pilgrims (but NOT Hindu or foreign tourists) were polluting the Himalayas and cutting down trees. This all was leading to the receding of glaciers and causing GLOBAL WARMING, they claimed.

The Governor being the head of an ostensibly Hindu Shrine Board couldn't ignore the popular sentiments and pleaded with Mufti to relent. Mufti dilli-dallied till four Hindu ministers of his cabinet belonging to Congress *resigned*. The downfall of his government was now imminent. Mufti had to give in, but he was seething from within.

As Chief Minister, he retaliated by ordering a total *non-cooperation* from his field agencies. The police were *ordered* to stop all supplies, including prefabricated toilets, going for the yatra. Mr. I.C. Jandial, the then-Development Commissioner, of SASB was physically *barred* from going to the yatra route and in fact made to sit in a police station for *four hours*. On enquiry from the Divisional Commissioner, Arun was told that since SASB *owned no* land on the pilgrimage route, it *couldn't* be permitted to erect even toilets!

This was strange logic. If pilgrims were polluting the environment, then measures like toilets and waste management facilities were necessary to reduce that pollution. Also, if State Government for decades could make these arrangements on the same route without bothering to acquire any land, why couldn't a government created body like SASB do the same?

The upshot was that SASB had to apply formally to the Forest Department for permission to install temporary structures all over the yatra route for those two months. And guess who had to process this "anti-Kashmir" request in the Forest Department?

Yours truly, because I was then in the chair of the Forest Secretary!

As per procedure, I sent SASB's request to the Principal Chief Conservator of Forests (PCCF), who marked it down to the Chief Conservator of Forests (CCF), who sent it down to the DFO and so on. By the time any reply trickled back, the 2-month yatra of 2004 was over. In any case, the report I received back was that to process the SASB request, a detailed survey had to be conducted which because of the oncoming winter months was not possible. *That was typical government-speak, when you want to do nothing!*

Okay, could we then give the Shrine Board "temporary permission" for the duration of the yatra for the next year? Yes, this could be permissible under rules, opined the CCF through the PCCF in writing. I accordingly made out a note and sent it to the minister in charge of forests (a Kashmiri Muslim) for his approval.

After he agreed, the Forest Department issued an order giving *temporary permission* to the Amarnath Shrine Board to set up facilities for two months. We put in a lot of conditions like no trees would be cut, the soil cover would not be disturbed, and the whole area would be cleaned up after the yatra was over, etc.

For the 2005 yatra, when prefab toilets were being taken to the camp sites, Mufti again asked the Divisional Commissioner Kashmir to stop them. But this time SASB staff were armed with the temporary approval given by the Forest Department.

Taking advantage of the confusion, Arun went ahead at break neck speed to ensure that all foul-smelling deep trench latrines, that were being put up for years together by state agencies, were replaced wholesale by more than 2000 prefabricated but modern water closets. These with the use of a special Japanese microbial technology, not only eliminated malodour, but also converted the sewage into compost on the spot.

Arun also introduced over 200 insulated, prefabricated huts, many with attached toilets, and 45 shelter sheds, all over the route that were a boon for pilgrims in bad weather. Water filters, supply of hot water through gas geysers, a formidable grill to protect the holy Ice-lingam from tampering and human interference, and a non-stop dawn-to-dusk helicopter service—that was unique in the world in its intensity of operations were some of his other achievements worth mentioning here.

Mufti was *furious*. He called Arun for a dressing down and *specifically* asked him to stop the helicopter services forthwith. This was interesting because helicopters had made the shrine accessible to *rich* pilgrims which disproved the *myth* that only sadhus and beggars were going on this yatra creating pollution and nuisance in the process.

Anyway, Arun respectively submitted that civil aviation being a subject dealt with the Central Government, he had already taken all due permissions. Also, that he was only extending a service to pilgrims which was already available in Vaishno Devi. At this Mufti *exploded* and said that "that was in Jammu and this is *Kashmir*!"

When Arun reported the matter to the Governor, the latter refused to relent. So, Mufti *banned* SASB's helicopter operations from the Nehru Helipad in Srinagar. The helicopters then started operating from the Srinagar Airport that was under the control of the Government of India.

Mufti then used the Nehru Helipad for operating the state helicopter on the same route to Amarnath. But the state pilot became so *greedy* that he started *pocketing* the fare himself and *ignored* routine maintenance and his own mandated medical check-ups. One day the state helicopter *crashed* killing the pilot and all passengers aboard. The resultant furore and enquiries made Mufti beat a hasty retreat and helicopter operations to the Amarnath shrine thereafter faced no obstructions from the State Government.

But that couldn't stop Mufti from *bad-mouthing* General Sinha and complaining to his Congress allies who were now in power in the Government of India to remove him. The Governor on the other hand was relentless in sending extremely negative reports on the blatantly communal shenanigans of the Chief Minister.

Apprehending that Mufti's "anti-Hindu" stand would strengthen BJP's poll prospects in the country, the Congress High Command didn't approve giving Mufti a second three-year tenure as CM. Instead in November 2005, they parachuted

Mr. Ghulam Nabi Azad, who was not even a member of the legislature in J&K, as the CM.

Anyway, unwittingly I was caught in the centre of the *storm* unleashed by the dislike and disdain of the Governor and the CM towards each other. *Naturally it was time for me to be changed, again!*

This time the seniority norm was not followed and a very *junior* promoted officer was sent in my place. *So much for the blah-blah about the sanctity of the seniority and morale of an All-India Service like the Indian Forest Service!*

And I was shifted as the Principal Secretary Health and Medical Education.

Chapter 18

In the Quagmire of Health and Medical Education

MY TENURE IN the Health and Medical Education department began on a very dramatic note. The minister Suman Lata Bhagat of the Congress was not present in the cabinet meeting when this decision to transfer me was taken. Considering my no-nonsense reputation, she apprehended that she would be unable to browbeat me into accepting any of her corrupt, illegal or unreasonable dictates. In any case, the department was run by her son who was otherwise a government servant, in fact, a junior engineer in the PWD department.

Dealing with Suman Lata Bhagat

ON THE FIRST day of joining, I received three "chits" (scribbles on half page slips) from the minister. One wanted me to transfer Director Health Kashmir and post another doctor in his place. The second was to post a junior non-gazetted officer as Deputy Controller of Drugs. The third was to transfer some doctors from one place to another.

I complied with the third wish as this could be done under rules and was within the competence of the minister. As for the other two, I *pasted* her chits on proper office files and sent up my views.

Regarding the first issue, I pointed out that the power to transfer Director Health, who is a state-level officer, lay only with the cabinet and asked the minister whether I should accordingly make out a proposal for the cabinet. Regarding the second, I wrote that NO rules permitted a non-gazetted officer to hold a gazetted post and so the request just *couldn't* be carried out.

The minister was furious. She rang me up and *screamed* on the phone, "What am I then minister for? Should I resign?"

I kept my cool and said,

"Madam, in the government set-up, we all have *limitations*, and no one has unbridled power. As for resigning that can be solely your personal decision and I cannot comment on the same."

This was not the beginning I had hoped for but I had little choice. After a while, the minister, in her own manner, tried to wave a white flag. She called me to her room and said that it didn't look nice when two l*adies* fight.

I readily nodded my head in agreement but what she said next *zapped* me.

She said, "Why don't you have a setting with me then? You do a few of my works and I'll do yours."

And, in other words, we could both happily share the booty. I didn't know what to say for a second. And also, didn't know how to say it. Or that I even heard the word "setting" correctly.

When I could finally gather my wits, I had to tell her that I had no personal agenda or relatives to oblige. Further as an administrator in my official capacity I was duty bound to dispense justice to *all* on the merits of each individual case. So, this great "setting" concept was totally unacceptable to me.

While all this was going on, I as usual went about my job with all the dedication at my command. The National Rural Health Mission had been just launched in the country but was nowhere in sight in J&K. So, I prepared the file personally and started working on the intricacies of its implementation in the state.

I also began working on the long-pending promotion issues of doctors and the staff of the medical colleges. There was a decision—that since doctors do the same work all their lives, though in different capacities, they should be given *time-bound* promotions. A system of three time-bound promotions was instituted. But—what happened next was—that only the first and second promotions were given out quite in routine. For the third, the whole *pick and choose* attitude of J&K kicked in.

So far only three doctors, who were considered *close* to the powers that be, could earn this third time-bound promotion. I had a *detailed* re-look at the cabinet note in which the original order had been approved and realised that the third time-bound promotion too—could be given to all eligible doctors. I, therefore, ordered its immediate implementation *without* referring it to anyone else.

This one step lifted the morale of government doctors as nothing could. Till date, doctors continue to thank me for what they term as a *revolutionary* order. As the order made the promotions applicable from the date they were due, even those doctors who had retired (or were dead) benefitted as it made a big difference to their pensions.

Another very interesting incident took place during this period. I got a note from the minister one day that a government order should be issued assigning a particular work in the Dental College Srinagar to a junior assistant working there. I immediately wrote back stating that the Principal of the Dental College was fully *competent* to decide which of his clerical staff should deal with what subject, and as the administrative department, we should not be interfering in such matters. The minister, however, insisted that we still *should* issue a government order.

I then sent up a note to the CM outlining my viewpoint and asked for his directions. Thankfully, the CM agreed with me and *no* government order had to be issued.

And Getting the Boot

BUT THAT WAS not the end of the matter. Almost every day, there would be some unpleasant exchange. Finally, I had to tell Ms. Bhagat that if she didn't like my *style* of working, she could get me transferred. But till I sat on the chair, I was the Principal Secretary and I had to act only as per rules. The minister finally used her other Congress colleagues in the cabinet and much to my *relief*, I was transferred to the Revenue department.

My son had meanwhile secured admission for the LLB (Hons.) course in the University College London (where Tagore and Mahatma Gandhi once studied) and was leaving for the UK in September. I had become so madly busy in the Health and Medical Education department that I seemed to hardly have *any* time for my family. So, I happily took two months of leave and had an absolutely fabulous time relaxing at home.

What surprised me was the media war that ensued. Every day there were reports of the misdeeds of the minister and many reports praised me sky-high. It seems one had struck a chord somewhere in the hearts of the doctors and the common masses.

The Chief Secretary had meanwhile changed and Mr. Vijay Bakaya was the new CS. His ascendance was another interesting story. His batch mate Mr. Ajit Kumar (1970 IAS JK) was senior to him and much younger in age. But how could an "outsider" occupy such an exalted position?

So, all kinds of cases were *instituted* against Ajit Kumar. He was *arrested* and put in jail for some time. His pensionary benefits were withheld. Cases against him continue till date!

All competition to Mr. Bakaya was over. *And in there lay a message, warning "outsiders" of their fate if they ever crossed swords with a chosen son-of-the -soil.*

Anyway Mr. Bakaya felt that my being on leave was creating a grave embarrassment for the government, and so I should join back. I was in any case free. My son had left for the UK. Arun was busy in Raj Bhavan.

Shunted out to Revenue

SO, ON THE 3rd of October 2005, I joined as Principal Secretary in the Department of Revenue, Relief and Rehabilitation. I remember the date because we had a massive earthquake in Kashmir on the 8th of October, within five days of my joining.

Suddenly, this "dead department" was the centre of all activity. Things had to move fast. Fortunately, my earlier Health Department rose to the occasion like nothing could. Within *four hours* of the earthquake, doctors had reached Uri. There was no outbreak of any disease.

There was not a single death directly connected with the earthquake, unlike just 10 km across the border in Pakistan where *hundreds* had perished. All injured were looked after well. In fact, the civilian doctors extended help to the army medical teams as well in places like Tangdhar where the Army Hospital had collapsed.

The month of October saw another change. As per the understanding between the Congress and the PDP, the Chief Minister's position was to rotate between PDP and Congress. Mufti's three-year regime was coming to an end; so it was Congress' turn to nominate its CM. Mufti, however, was trying his *best* to carry on for another three years. As an old Congress hand himself, he had almost convinced Sonia Gandhi that letting him *rule* meant rule of the Congress itself.

I learnt that Mufti was sponsoring different groups of journalists, craftspeople, lawyers, businessmen, etc. to convince the Congress leadership to allow Mufti to continue as "Kashmir really needed him." In fact, on the 22nd of October 2005, when his continuance was expected to be announced, Mufti had planned to hold a media conference at 4 p.m.

But here I think the negative reports sent by the Governor prevailed and Ghulam Nabi Azad was declared the CM. Subsequently, Mr. Azad was sworn in at Srinagar in the beginning of November.

I had known Mr. Azad from the time he had come to Leh as Union Minister of Food in 1987. And thereafter when he would visit Sitaram Kesari when I was in the Ministry of Welfare. We had an interesting interaction with him in Leh when he had come to Leh to campaign for the Congress candidate contesting the state elections.

Although he was a union cabinet minister, Arun as DC decided—that since Mr. Azad was basically coming for a political purpose—it would be improper to receive him at the airport and so *didn't*. Mind you, there was *no* model code of conduct imposed by the Election Commission in those days mandating such an action. Yet, and very surprisingly, Mr. Azad was *gracious* enough to understand Arun's logic. In fact, he floored us by sending us a carton of luscious Alphonso mangoes he had carried from Delhi.

We then called on him at the circuit house, next to the DC's house, where he was staying. Arun also decided to escort him on Mr. Azad's official inspection of the stores of the Food Corporation of India after the campaigning was over.

Now as CM, when we met at the tea hosted in his honour at the Raj Bhavan, he recognised me and after the usual pleasantries asked me *point blank* about the "magic wand" that I had waved over the doctors.

"Sonali ji, what is this? If I get my blood pressure measured, the doctor requests me to get you back as Principal Secretary Health. And if I have a tooth problem, it is the same story. And this is repeated whenever I meet any doctor of any discipline," said Mr. Azad.

He then added with a smile, "If you were a *state subject*, I would have made you the Health Minister."

Back to Health

TRUE TO HIS impressions, in the first cabinet meeting that Azad held, he transferred me back to the Health Department. Not only that, assessing the importance of this department in public mind, he kept this portfolio with himself. So, he was now the CM as well as my Health Minister.

The welcome I got this time was literally like the proverbial return of the prodigal. Arun and I were having our usual evening walk in the park adjoining our house in Jammu when a crowd started building up on the road outside the house. We thought *maybe there was some function in the adjoining house.*

But when we came back, I realised that the sea of humanity comprised all kinds of doctors who had come to greet me with sweets. I thanked them all but refused the sweets.

Next day, I issued a circular that no one should come to my house without prior appointment and that too in an emergency only. Doctors are *busy people* and they should *rather* be *saving* lives than greeting their Principal Secretary with sweets.

Back in the chair, I was *sad* to see that the file on National Rural Health Mission (NRHM)—that was being implemented everywhere else in the country—was just growing nice and fat with *no* results. The inertia had to be broken. So, I wrote a six-page note in my longhand outlining the action that needed to be taken for its implementation. This became the very foundation of the scheme in J&K.

In the first review meeting that Mr. Azad took, he asked me about the NRHM file as the Union Minister of Health had spoken to him about it. He was happy to find that the file was already there in his section and approved it immediately.

We focussed on improving the health infrastructure and work began in right earnest from the sub-centres to the district hospitals. It was also during this period that two super specialty hospitals—one each for Jammu and Srinagar were sanctioned. The new children's hospital in Badami Bagh became functional.

The up-gradation of the main maternity hospital in Srinagar started. The dental college and hospital in Jammu also became functional. Homoeopathy as a branch of medicine was introduced with a separate cadre for the first time in J&K. And *at last*, Ayurvedic, Yunani, Siddha and Homoeopathy (AYUSH) became an integral part of the health initiative in J&K.

The problem now facing us was the posting of doctors. Any doctor posted to a far-flung area would immediately get a stay from the courts and happily continue with his private practice in Jammu/Srinagar.

It so happened that I met Justice Bashir Ahmed Khan, the Chief Justice of J&K High Court, at a social gathering. He had heard of my initiatives and told me that everyone had high expectations now that I was back heading the Health Department. I saw a window of opportunity at that praise and requested him to help me.

"Help you? How?" He was taken aback.

I told him about the problem of "stay orders" given by various courts and lamented how I could NOT then post any doctor to any far-flung area. It was unbelievable what followed next. The Chief Justice, the very next day *suo motu* and rather unilaterally vacated all stay orders of doctors. Wow!

I suddenly had over 200 doctors to post and I did not waste a minute. I made out a proposal and got it approved by the Chief Minister/Health Minister. While posting doctors out, I also took care to get some doctors who had spent more than adequate *time* in far-off areas to Jammu/Srinagar.

These two hundred doctors were extremely well connected and the pressure to retain them in Jammu/Srinagar started to build up. Mr. Azad's Principal Secretary asked me to put up the case of a recently transferred doctor but I insisted on carrying the file myself to the CM. I requested Mr. Azad that he should not change the transfer order of even one doctor as this would open a Pandora's Box and he would ultimately need to post each one back. Mr. Azad listened intently and agreed to let all the doctors remain at their ordered posts of duty.

The concept of health in J&K so far was only on the *treatment* of disease. We managed to introduce the concept of *wellness* instead and in this—all branches of medicine including Ayurveda and Homoeopathy were to play a major role.

Another problem was that various departments in the Medical College Srinagar were getting de-recognised by the Medical Council of India (MCI) due to a *lack* of teaching staff whereas in Jammu there was *over-staffing*. There was a common seniority for Jammu Medical College and Srinagar Medical College all right. But the problem was that the doctors especially in Jammu had well established private practices. So, although they wanted to take the promotion and the grade, they were unwilling to move to Srinagar where the vacancies lay. A piquant situation had, therefore, arisen that I couldn't tolerate.

So, I ordered that the doctors either join at their new posts or forego their promotion. This worked for some time but soon this powerful lobby moved the politicians. To *avoid* going to Srinagar, they came up with the idea to split the seniority list, region wise, so that Jammu doctors could stay in Jammu and Kashmir ones in Srinagar. Despite my opposition, the issue was *cleared* by the cabinet. The result was that *while the doctors in Kashmir received accelerated promotions, Jammu was gripped by stagnation.*

Purchasing medicines was another issue which we managed to streamline. I was happy to note that at all district level review meetings headed by the Chief Minister, the MLAs and other people's representatives actually praised the working of the Health Department. Otherwise, this department used to get the maximum bashing.

Gurez-Tilel is an adjacent valley to the Kashmir valley. It gets cut off for over six months during the winter. I wanted to ensure that *adequate* medical facilities should be available to the population there. I, therefore, decided to go there along with all my heads of departments.

I also sent in advance a medical team of eye surgeons to the sub-district hospital at Dawar, Gurez. The population of the area is not much. So, I wanted this team to perform cataract operations on all needy persons to help declare the entire valley *cataract free*. The medical team camped there for a month and was able to *fulfil* this objective.

When I reached Gurez, at the sub-district hospital, I *couldn't believe* what I was seeing. For the first time in the history of Gurez, ten specialist doctors were treating patients and conducting surgeries of all kind. The MLA of the area Mr. Nazir Gurezi joined me and stated that he had never seen this hospital so full of activity. All I had done was to post doctors who belonged to this area and who had taken advantage of getting medical seats because of this fact of belonging to a backward area.

The MLA, however, said that the NRHM was *not* working in that area. We were standing in a village. So, I decided to ascertain what the truth was, then and there. My Director Health Kashmir had told me that ASHAs (Accredited Social Health Activists) had been selected for each village and were all under training. So, I asked the villagers who was their ASHA. At first, they looked blank. And then their faces lit up, "Oh the village lady who is to help us in medical situations—call Ruksana."

The MLA was surprised because the selection of ASHAs had been done in a totally decentralised manner with the help of the community and by keeping politicians like him away. That's why he had no idea!

There was no mobile connection in this area. So, I was happily touring village to village without knowing what was awaiting me.

When we reached Razdan pass, which leads to Kashmir, the mobiles came to life. And I saw all my HODs suddenly looking quite upset. "What happened?" I asked.

Calamity, of course. I was *thrown out* of the Health department. Transferred only after 8 months!

All my HODs were blaming themselves. They felt that had they been in Srinagar, they would not have allowed this transfer to happen. I learnt I was transferred because I was "arrogant."

That I was, I suppose. Because only an "arrogant" person could ignore all *sifarish* (requests) and dare post doctors with powerful connections to serve poor people in far-flung areas!

Chapter 19

In the "Dog House" of Administrative Reforms

THIS TIME I was banished to the Administrative Reforms and Inspections (ARI) Department, which was literally the "dog house" of the secretariat. Anything that made you important—staff to transfer, vehicles to let your relatives and guests roam in, projects to rake in commissions—was missing in this department!

These things, of course, *didn't* matter to me, but after the hectic work of the Health Department, administrative reforms did feel extremely *staid*. In a state with the *worst* kind of administration, what kind of reforms was I supposed to initiate?

Anyway, once I sat down in my new office and pored over old files, I found to my *surprise* that most departments had no written down recruitment or promotion *rules*. And those who did have some had such antiquated ones that they made little sense.

So, I held detailed meetings with all "delinquent" department heads, and in the two years I spent in this department I managed to formulate and finalise rules of over 50 departments. This I believe was quite a record from the time the department was created!

Well, yes, only in the dungeon of a department like ARI could I last *full* two years. Normally, the harder I worked, and the more decisions I took, the faster I was transferred! But NOT from ARI.

I never called on Mr. Azad formally to complain about my fate. But interestingly, whenever I'd bump into him in some function or another he would do "tut...tut" and tell me how I was being "wasted" in ARI and how industrialists wanted me back in the Industries Department and doctors in the Health Department, and so on. He himself wanted me to come back to the Revenue Department to make a scheme called "Roshni."

The idea was to *legalise* the ownership of all those who had grabbed government land *illegally*. And to use the fees earned from such a "regularisation" to pay for the state's massive electricity dues that it owed to many non-J&K power companies. So, you legitimise one illegal act, of encroaching state land, to help gloss over another, of not paying your electricity bills! This was something totally against my ethics and so I refused to even discuss the idea.

Sadly, this "Roshni" scheme was still pushed through and nowadays is a huge *scandal* with probes started by the Comptroller and Auditor General of India, the Vigilance Organisation, the High Court, and so on.

Moving to Agriculture

MEANWHILE, THE Agriculture and Horticulture Minister Mr. Zargar and Mr. Dilawar Mir respectively wanted me to become the Agriculture Production Commissioner (APC). Mr. Azad being a Congress man initially resisted as he did not want to give "a good officer" to PDP ministers. He didn't, however, mind "wasting a good officer" in his own words in ARI! Anyway, after almost two years of dilly dallying, he gave in and posted me as APC in February 2008.

A little credit for this, of course, goes to the new Chief Secretary, Mr. B.R. Kundal, who didn't indeed wish to *waste* good officers in peripheral departments. The upshot was that I landed up in the Agriculture Department with the charge of Horticulture and Floriculture as well.

2008 was to be one of the most dramatic of the years I had spent so far in J&K. The year began on the usual note. The earlier APC had not even released Plan Funds to the various departments under his charge. So, I had to redress that first. Then there were issues of fertilizer availability, monitoring of the National Horticulture Mission which was performing abysmally and other related matters.

Both my ministers were easy to work with and supported me to the hilt. The *Rashtriya Krishi Vikas Yojna* (The National Agriculture Development Mission) had *not* been extended to J&K. With a lot of homework, and hard work I was able to convince the central Planning Commission and the Agriculture Ministry to extend it to J&K. My success was received with much fanfare in J&K.

Meanwhile politics took a strange turn. Mr. Kundal resigned as Chief Secretary, joined the Congress Party, and the next day was made a Cabinet Minister for Finance and Planning. Once more, the debate of having outsider *versus* insider for the post of CS began.

With an "anti-outsider" like Mufti no longer in saddle, I relentlessly campaigned in favour of following *seniority*, lest officers like me simply lose heart. Surprisingly, both my ministers were convinced and with them arguing for him, Mr. S.S. Kapur (1974 IAS JK) was made Chief Secretary. However, what a horror he would turn out to be, acting more loyal than the king? But that could emerge only after a while.

General Sinha's term as a Governor came to an end in June 2008. Although the Prime Minister personally promised him a 3-month extension till the elections were over, it did not happen. And Mr. N.N. Vohra arrived on the scene.

The Amarnath Bomb Explodes

THIS WAS THE election year in J&K and all political parties were looking for *contentious* issues to help win the election. Meanwhile, harassed by Mufti's attitude to the Amarnath pilgrimage, the SASB had formally applied to the State Government to allot some land to them.

The cabinet headed by Mr. Azad, with the concurrence of the Deputy Chief Minister and Law Minister Mr. Muzaffar Baig and Mr. Qazi Afzal, the Forest Minister (both from PDP) cleared the long pending request of the Amarnath Shrine Board and sanctioned some land at Baltal, near Sonemarg, for creating temporary facilities for pilgrims.

This was exploited to the hilt by the separatists, communalists and the anti-national elements. The land allotment was made out to be a *sell-out* of Kashmiri interests. The PDP which was a party to this decision took a *"holier than thou"* attitude and withdrew from the government. Street protests, stone-throwing, anti-India slogans became a daily occurrence.

When Mr. Vohra arrived in Srinagar as the new Governor, the leaders of all Kashmir centric political parties met him and told him to "return the land" allotted to the Amarnath Shrine Board. Arun was still the Principal Secretary to Governor as well as the CEO SASB. He flew back with Mr. Vohra in the state plane and gave him a detailed briefing. He also requested the Governor NOT to take a decision in a hurry. There were ways of NOT accepting the land especially when the Shrine Board had to pay about Rupees 2.50 crores (25 million) as compensation to the State Government which it could ill-afford.

But all anti-national parties had left their goons on the streets and this was quite a scary time. They were also *blaming* Arun for claiming in a press conference that Muslim pollution in Kashmir was worse than the Hindu pollution (caused by pilgrims), when he actually had quoted the popular press reports to this effect and debunked them by terming these as "nonsensical."

Mr. Vohra wanting to be *popular* wrote a letter to the CM "returning" the land. He also changed Arun as his Principal Secretary and asked B.B. Vyas (1986 IAS JK) to replace him—on a Sunday morning. Arun had lasted with Mr. Vohra precisely for two days!

"Returning" the land pleased nobody. PDP still went on to pull the rug under Mr. Azad's feet. Losing his majority in the Legislature, he had no option but to put in his papers. And the state went under Governor's Rule.

Kashmir quietened down a bit, but as Arun had warned—Jammu turned volatile. I remember Mr. S.S. Kapur who had "attached" Arun to the GAD telling us that there will be some drama of an enquiry about what Arun said or didn't. But as for Jammu, he said,

"Who cares for Jammu? These guys can be handled easily."

Kapur was so very wrong this time. The anger in Jammu was so strong that even women belonging to respectable, upper class families were coming out on the streets to break the curfew. The security forces felt helpless as the ladies were tying *rakhis* (friendship bands) on their hands, shouting *Bharat Mata ki jai* (Long live Mother India) and waving the National Flag.

Kashmiris were aghast that the police were NOT beating up the protesters in Jammu the way they did in Kashmir. But as I joked, the Kashmiris also had the option of shouting *Bharat Mata ki jai* and waving the National Flag which they were not exercising!

Just then, Mr. Omar Abdullah gave a speech in Parliament saying *inter alia* that Kashmiris will die but "not yield even an inch of land (to outsiders)." Interestingly, the debate was about the desirability of having a nuclear agreement with US and this comment was totally uncalled for. This statement went viral on social media and added fuel to fire. One person in Jammu committed suicide declaring in public that he could also lay down his life for the Amarnath land if that is what was required.

The police in their clumsy manner tried to dispose of the body by cremating it quietly. The "plans" leaked out, and the situation took a hideous turn. In fact, for the first-time in recent history, Jammu people who have very strong business ties with Kashmir, decided that they would counter the blatantly communal attitude of Kashmiris by imposing an economic blockade on the latter.

This was unprecedented. The separatists reacted by suggesting that they should sell their apples "via Muzaffarabad," in Pak-occupied J&K which in any case was the traditional land-route to Punjab in pre-1947 era. The police allowed them to proceed, to "let their steam off," as a senior Indian Police Service officer advised. *There was no political will to engage with anyone telling them how wrong they were to oppose a centuries' old pilgrimage to Amarnath in the first place.* There were just "Band-Aid" kind of measures and counter-measures, appeasement, and more appeasement.

The result was ghastly. One separatist was assassinated by his rivals while taking part in the march to Muzaffarabad. The Indian security agencies were blamed and what followed thereafter were more curfews and *hartals* and marauders roaming on the streets.

Going to office each day became a nightmare. On the streets of Srinagar, you would have hordes of motorcyclists coming from the wrong direction—three on each bike, with green bands tied around their heads, and shouting, *"Azadi Azadi Azadi Allahu Akbar."*

My bindi and sari were glared at and on one occasion my driver who was a Kashmiri Muslim himself asked me to remove my bindi lest we got into trouble. After all, in the vehicle, there was only one Personal Security Officer (PSO), my driver and myself. What could we possibly do if the mob attacked us?

It struck me that the last time I had to remove my bindi was—in Pakistan!

Hitting Back at Arun

IN JAMMU, THE effigy of Mr. Vohra was burnt each day which really angered him. Poor Arun was kept without a posting. The house we were occupying was in the annexe of the Raj Bhavan. We were ready to vacate but needed alternate accommodation.

I spoke to Mr. B.B. Vyas, the Principal Secretary to Governor, and also to his wife who readily agreed that I could continue to stay till I was given some other accommodation. In any case, Vyas lived right across in the *Cheshma Shahi* JKTDC Huts, and claimed to be reasonably happy there.

With great difficulty, Srinagar and Jammu finally limped back to normalcy but Arun and I were made the *villain* of the piece. I, because, I had given permission for setting up temporary shelters way back in 2005.

And Arun because he had tried to explain the need for erecting those temporary facilities to tackle pollution and to save precious lives.

Also, he had warned that Jammu may go up in flames if Mr. Vohra wrote that letter himself for returning the land. And since that was what exactly happened in Jammu, so naturally Arun was the villain!

Anyway, I carried on with my official work. I was able to finalise the seniority list of departments like Horticulture and Sericulture but the main Agriculture Department was in an absolute mess. No proper promotions had taken place over 30 years and total *ad-hocism* prevailed. There were about 10-15 officials in the department in a list of about 900 who were benefitting from this chaos.

I had meetings with different groups and strictly following the prevalent recruitment rules, we drew up a seniority list and accordingly proposed promotions subject to confirmations by the Public Service Commission (PSC) which was required under rules.

The note was approved by the Advisor Mr. H.H. Tyabji (1965 IAS JK)—yes, the earlier Chief Secretary and the then Agricultural Production Commissioner who was now the Advisor to the Governor. He had no love lost for me but appreciated the hard work which had gone in leading to the resolution on this tricky problem.

He supported my proposal in glowing terms and when the note went up to the Governor, he also approved. Mr. Vohra in fact wrote that in case there were such issues in other departments they should also take similar action.

Things were, however, going from bad to worse at home. Suddenly, on the 30th of September, Arun was served with an eviction notice by the Governor's Secretariat asking us to vacate our house by 8 P.M. on the 1st of October, that was the next day. I may mention here that by the end of October, in any case, we would have vacated as we would be required to move to Jammu in the annual "Darbar move."

My hands went cold, and I was worried beyond words. *Where were we supposed to go with all our luggage?* It was Governor's Rule after all and the Governor, if he wanted to help, could have very well allotted us a suitable house that we would have moved to immediately.

Once again, our Kashmiri friends came in handy. They came to our house and got Arun to simply sign on a blank piece of paper. They typed on it a petition about our plight and presented it to the court of Judge Hasnain Masoodi, the District and Sessions Judge Srinagar, the next day. The Judge "stayed" the Governor's order giving us some time to pack our belongings and move to Jammu (where we did have government accommodation) by the 20th of October, which is what we wanted.

Such defiance of the Governor's orders during Governor's Rule was unheard of in J&K. Mr. Vohra was furious and now we knew he will hit back even harder.

Arun had not been given a posting now for over 4 months and so he went to Jammu, engaged a lawyer and moved the Central Administrative Tribunal (CAT). The moment he did that, Vohra blinked and posted Arun as Principal Secretary, Information Technology (IT) Department.

This was one of the most *insignificant* of all departments in J&K and was in fact carved out of the bigger Science and Technology Department especially for Arun. He was now required to take charge of a "part of a department" from an officer who was 14 years his junior. Anyway, this is how J&K works. *We couldn't help notice that it is only in J&K where a department like IT or Science and Technology is considered the most insignificant!*

The problem was that we now had NO house in Srinagar. So, we had to stay in the State Guest House and pay through our nose for our board and lodge till the offices closed in Srinagar and we could move to Jammu. A typical "outsider's fate," I suppose.

Arrives Mr. Omar Abdullah

ELECTIONS HAD BEEN announced, and the results threw up a hung assembly. The PDP with all the furore they had created against the Amaranth Yatra did not do too well. The National Conference which had fought under the leadership of Farooq Abdullah had performed better. Congress too got a beating in the Jammu region and for the first-time BJP won 11 seats riding on the pro-Amarnath wave in Jammu.

A Congress-NC combined was soon cobbled up. An evening before the swearing in, Mr. Farooq Abdullah had declared to Barkha Dutt, the NDTV journalist that he was taking over as the CM the next day. But surprise, surprise!

It was Mr. Omar Abdullah who was sworn-in instead. There are stories of a family coup where Sachin Pilot (who is Farooq Abdullah's son-in-law) and Farooq's wife supported

Omar Abdullah but no one can verify what really transpired during that night before the "coronation."

Mr. Omar Abdullah's Government was sworn in January 2009. I was happy that now that we had a young dynamic Chief Minister, he could take the State to new heights of development. This illusion was somewhat shattered in the very first official meeting I had with Omar.

I had prepared a detailed presentation of the agriculture, horticulture, sericulture, floriculture and command area projects I was dealing with. Within minutes of the start of my presentation, Omar, the CM, started playing with his mobile.

I noticed he had the same "engrossed" look on his face that my son has while playing "Angry birds!" And lo-and-behold, after about five minutes, Omar lost his patience and said he will review the sector next time. This "next time" of course never came till I was there for another year.

I had two cabinet ministers Mr. Sham Lal Sharma, in charge of horticulture and related sectors, and Mr. Ghulam Hassan Mir, in charge of agriculture and related subjects. The interesting fact about Mr. Mir was that though he did not belong to either the Congress or the National Conference, he was made a cabinet minister. Rumours were that it was probably on the behest of some intelligence agencies who had "invested" in him deeply.

The rumours were confirmed when a few years later, General (Retd.) V.K. Singh, who was Chief of the Indian Army, thanked Mir for his "co-operation" in one of his speeches. This led to a furore in the press and even in J&K's legislature who issued a notice to General Singh to come and explain his "allegations."

Nothing much came out of all that sound and fury but what surprised me was that Mr. Mir was virulently against *all Kashmiris whose hearts, minds and souls were with India.* He would go out of his way to trouble and harm them. I suppose this was so because Mir wanted to project that he could be the only true ally and confidante of India in Kashmir. His coffers should always be kept full; otherwise the cause of India was lost in Kashmir!

I brought this to the notice of my friends in the Intelligence Bureau but it didn't seem to cut much ice.

"All Kashmiri politicians are corrupt," they would say dismissively.

"But he is the most dangerous," I would reiterate and share with them my impression of how he was undermining all-other pro-India forces in Kashmir.

My feedback at last had some effect. Mir's funding was finally reduced, and he lost elections in 2014.

As for me, Mr. Mir had a lot of problems. He did not like the fact that I was slowly doing away with the rampant *ad-hocism* in the Agriculture Department. Government of India was generously funding the National Agriculture Development Scheme (*Rashtriya Krishi Vikas Yojna),* but the funds were for a specific purpose.

Mr. Mir wanted to spend money only on "soil conservation" which is a *big racket* in J&K where huge amounts of money are spent with no accountability and nothing to show on ground. Money straight into the pockets of all concerned. I, of course, was certainly not agreeable to this, and "soil conservation" in any case was not included in the approved list of items that could be taken up under the national scheme. This annoyed Mir no end.

The Perfidy of Kapur

WITH ALL THIS political churning going on another story was unfolding at the administrative level. Mr. S.S. Kapur, as Chief Secretary, had appointed a three-member committee to enquire into Arun's conduct during his press conference in June 2008. Of the three, two were junior to Arun, and Arun had challenged this fact too in the Central Administrative Tribunal (CAT).

In May 2009, the CAT *struck down* this committee's prejudiced report and indicted the State Government in rather strong terms. Instead of accepting his wrong decision, Mr. Kapur only seemed to get angrier with Arun.

So quietly, in the month of November, when all of us were in Jammu because of the durbar move, Mr. Kapur moved the High Court of J&K at Srinagar and got it to *stay* the operation of the CAT judgement. The lawyer who appeared on behalf of the State Government was the relative of a staunch separatist. Arun didn't even get a notice.

Bewildered, Arun met Mr. Kapur and asked him what was he getting stayed? That juniors should again be asked to hold enquiry against seniors or that a person of Arun's seniority and experience shouldn't be given any appropriate assignment?

Kapur had *no* answer, but he had to please his masters. So, in January 2010, he shifted Arun from the IT Department and sent him off to the J&K Special Tribunal which was considered an even more insignificant posting. In doing that, he ensured that Arun is physically "thrown out" of the secretariat.

For personal reasons, I needed to be in Delhi to get my house constructed. Retirement was not too far away and as an *outsider* I couldn't possibly settle in J&K where I had no rights. I could not build a house, I couldn't educate my child in any technical sector, I did not even have a right to vote in the Assembly or even municipal elections. I, therefore, requested for my posting as PRC (Principal Resident Commissioner) to Delhi.

My request came as a manna from heaven for both Mr. Mir and Mr. Kapur. So, in January 2010, I was posted to Delhi but NOT as PRC but as Principal Secretary Coordination—a non-functional post. Anyway, at least I was in Delhi.

Meanwhile in J&K suddenly all hell was let loose. The Agriculture promotion order that I had got processed, and that was approved by the Governor in 2008 was suddenly found to be full of "discrepancies." Mr. Kapur ordered that I be charge sheeted, without any "show cause notice" served to me first, as per rules.

This meant that from now on, I would be denied my "vigilance clearance" and be called "a charge sheeted officer." More ominously, this implied that I would be denied *all* future promotions and even my pension once I retired. Mr. Kapur was now playing to the anti-India lobby in full form!

Funnily, when the case went up to the courts, the single bench of the High Court upheld the order I had issued in the Agriculture Department. So, Mr. Mir went in appeal to the double bench of the High Court. While all this was going on, my replies, my representations, my pleadings—all went unheard and I remained "charge sheeted."

The empanelment process to the Additional Secretary level in Government of India was now in progress. So, I went and met the Cabinet Secretary and the Secretary Department of Personnel and gave them written representations. Mir had meanwhile poisoned Omar Abdullah so much that on my annual confidential report, he downgraded the rating of 9.8 (out of 10) that my Horticulture Minister Mr. Sham Lal Sharma had given me, to a mere 7. And then he added as if he was tweeting, "Lacks officer like qualities."

In all of my over 30 years of service, at least this had never been said to me. I immediately represented asking for the reasons why and how had the Honourable CM come to such a conclusion. Omar didn't know how to substantiate his comment. So, the bureaucracy stepped in and the technical reply I got was that this was NOT an "adverse comment" but only an "advisory." The blot on my record remained and the Government of India which only goes on the basis of such record termed me "unfit" to hold any post in the centre.

In Arun's case too, the required vigilance clearance was *denied* because the State Government of Jammu and Kashmir reported that it was "contemplating" to institute some kind of an inquiry against him. Mr. Kapur knew very well how the empanelment process in the Government of India worked and had realised that since Arun's annual confidential reports in the Government of India as well as in the Governor's Secretariat were all *outstanding*, this was the only way of ensuring that he was NOT empanelled as an Additional Secretary.

So, the Additional Secretary empanelment process in 2010 came and went and we got left out. The same process was repeated when the empanelment exercise at the Secretary level was completed for our batch of officers in 2012-13.

My vigilance clearance was only given when the double bench of the High Court again *upheld* the validity of the order issued by me in the Agriculture Department. In Arun's case, the moment he could get his case transferred to the Jammu branch from Srinagar (where not a single hearing had taken place in over two years), the State Government of J&K *withdrew* its appeal from the High Court. But that was too late—everything was over by then and we were doomed to rot in J&K.

The indifference of the Cabinet Secretary to our woes was unimaginable. *I realised how alone you are in this fight against anti-nationalism, communalism, corruption and gender insensitivity.* Hint of a controversy, the need to take a stand, the requirement of initiating a tough measure—and senior functionaries like Cabinet Secretary or Chief Secretary start quaking in their boots. The Government of India totally washes its hands of all responsibilities for abandoned creatures like us. They can spend millions in supposedly controlling militancy but will not lift their little finger to help those who could make all the difference.

It was darkness all around us. Once again.

Chapter 20

Rotting in Delhi

MY OFFICIAL WORK as Principal Secretary Coordination was negligible. I was given no personal staff and had to share my personal assistant with the common pool. So, I got involved in a lot of activities outside the office.

I became the coordinator for organising the 1979 IAS batch get together every month. I got involved with the setting up of the CSOI (Civil Services Officers' Institute) that was coming up in Chanakyapuri at Vinay Marg and got nominated as a member of its executive committee.

Most importantly, I first became a member of the executive body and then was elected as Secretary of the Greater Noida based Greenwood Officers' Welfare Society where I was planning to settle down.

This Society had been created to meet the housing need of Class I government service officers like us. In its Phase-I, it had distributed plots, which I didn't seek because I didn't think I could get anything constructed on it sitting in J&K.

In its Phase II, flats and villas were to be built by the Society itself. That suited the requirement of those officers like us who were posted far away.

The Society was being run by Mr. Harminder Raj Singh (IAS 1978 UP), who was then a Joint Secretary in the Home Ministry. A suave and smooth talking officer, he drove us to the site himself and impressed us with his vision of the Society. He then persuaded us to take a bank loan and pay up in full for our villa.

Carrying the "outsider's curse" on our drooping shoulders, we knew we could never have a house of our own in J&K. So we paid up, as advised, and returned to J&K hoping that may be in a few years we will have a home in the National Capital Region (NCR).

Harminder Raj in any case was the be all and end all of this Society. Little did I then know that the contractor chosen to complete our villas (and flats) was Harminder's brother-in-law and the architect his sister-in-law. The aim of the trio was obviously far from altruistic.

Our dream of having a roof over our heads was rudely shattered when we learnt that Harminder had committed suicide. There were whispers that actually he was killed by the land mafia because as Housing Secretary in Uttar Pradesh he had somehow *rubbed* them the wrong way.

Anyway, the total mess in the Society became obvious only after his death. We were amongst the worst sufferers as not even the ground floor of our villa was completed till then. The villa was to be handed over to us by 2005 and this was now 2010. My coming to Delhi was, therefore, absolutely essential to rescue this only property that we owned anywhere in the world.

I realised that not only me but numerous other officers were suffering because of this scam. Anyway, I am happy to say that we made the best of a terrible situation and with concerted effort sorted out most of the mess. In fact, when I bid the Society members goodbye as I had to join back in J&K, I was cheered in the AGM and everyone came and shook hands with me. In fact, some had tears in their eyes when they said they were hoping I would be back soon.

Mr. Madhav Lal (1977 IAS JK) became Chief Secretary in January 2011. And though my posting hadn't changed,

I am thankful that he realised the *stupidity* of all those cases instituted against both of us and got them all closed. We could now be given our belated promotion to our "fixed scale"—the maximum grade that any IAS officer can hope for. We shall be eternally grateful to Madhav for taking that initiative.

But Madhav's heart, like any outsider, was not in J&K, but in Delhi where his daughters were studying and his wife Suruchi was teaching in the prestigious school Sanskriti. Soon he managed to return to the Government of India and the next available senior in J&K Iqbal Khandey (IAS 1978) was made CS in 2013 by Omar Abdullah. This surprised many as—Omar's father Farooq Abdullah used to take the name of Iqbal publicly and abuse him. Iqbal's daughter had fought elections on a PDP ticket and Iqbal used to claim openly to be one of the creators of PDP.

There was a big sex scandal in 2005 in J&K in which scores of young girls were allegedly exploited sexually with the bait of giving them government jobs. The CBI (Central Bureau of Investigation) was called upon to investigate the case, and they found Iqbal, among many politicians and police men, involved in this racket.

In an unheard act bordering on drama, they intercepted Iqbal's official car on Gupkar Road in Srinagar, arrested him and put him in jail for almost six months. Iqbal was then heading the Planning and Development Department in the Secretariat, which is one of the most powerful posts in the state bureaucracy.

At that time, there was so much anger in Kashmir that the case had to be shifted to Chandigarh. Many of the exploited girls had deposed before a Magistrate implicating Iqbal. However, later all such victims and witnesses turned "hostile" and the CBI lost the case. For some strange reason (or because too many important people were involved in this case), CBI chose NOT to appeal to a higher court.

Meeting the Expenses of 7 Akbar Road

AND SO, MR. Khandey was now the Chief Secretary. In his first act of piety, he made me the Principal Resident Commissioner (PRC) in the rank of Financial Commissioner (equivalent to Chief Secretary). Earlier, all the PRCs had been much junior to me and I had to get used to being insulted and side-lined.

Just before my posting, the Additional Resident Commissioner was transferred and replaced by one Mr. Asif Khan. Asif was, like most highly connected persons in J&K, a total back door entrant in to government service. In 1990 when the Kashmir valley was in turmoil, Mr. Hamidullah Khan, a promoted IAS officer, had assisted Mr. Jagmohan in his second tenure as Governor. For this, his "pound of flesh" was that Asif, his useless, jobless son, be given a government job and posted as "Trade Agent Bombay," where no one would be any wiser of any recruitment rules being bent in the process. This was how Asif Khan got into government service and thereafter kept on rising because of his various connections.

As PRC, I was supposed to receive the Governor and CM whenever they came to Delhi. The Governor used to come about once a month but Mr. Omar Abdullah was in Delhi almost twice or thrice a week. I received him for the first time and then before he drove off in his Land Rover, I was told that I *shouldn't* bother to receive him as it "embarrasses" him.

The CM would stay at 5 Prithvi Raj Road, the official accommodation of the J&K Government. His suite was quite well done up according to his taste. However, his wife and son stayed at 7 Akbar Road, the official accommodation provided by the Government of India to the CM of J&K.

I had no problems with this arrangement except that as PRC I was supposed to meet the electricity, water, and all other expenses of 7 Akbar Road and that too *without* any formal authorisation. All expenditure on the stay of Mr. Omar Abdullah at J&K House was also met by the PRC office. I often wondered at the kind of bread and coffee Mr. Omar Abdullah liked because the bill would always be exceeding a couple of *thousands of rupees*! Anyway, this had all to be done because Omar was after all the Chief Minister.

But meeting the expenses of his family at 7 Akbar Road was much more problematic. After all, Mr. Omar Abdullah had officially declared that he and his wife were separated. Yet one day a gentleman very aggressively walked into my office room and declared,

"Madam is very angry with you."

"Now which madam is this?" I blinked.

"Madam CM."

"And who are you?" I asked.

"I am Narayan Swamy, PS (Private Secretary) to Chief Minister."

I had to blink again as I had never heard of this gentleman. On further enquiry, I gathered that Mr. Narayan Swamy was a clerk when Omar was a Minister of State in the Government of India in Industries and Commerce and that after his retirement he has been acting as a self-styled PS of Omar.

He even had a *stamp* of PS to CM. Since I was unaware of the existence of such a person, I asked the CM's office who he was and whether he was authorised to use the stamp of PS to CM.

The CM's office *denied* point blank that there was any such PS on their rolls. But what about the bills of 7 Akbar Road? Should my office pay that? If yes, under what authority?

The electricity and water bill and all kinds of purchases were coming to a lakh (100,000) of rupees a month and such a payment in my opinion could not be made *without* following proper procedure.

It was with great reluctance that CM's Secretariat authorised me to clear the bills. But obviously, my raising such "bureaucratic questions" was not making me popular with the "Madam."

Mr. Narayan Swamy also wanted me to get him an identity card from the Ministry of Civil Aviation to enable him to receive and see off "Madam" at the airport. This I flatly refused. So, Mr. Swamy left my office in a huff telling my orderly outside my office chambers that I would soon be *taught a lesson.*

The Biryani Episode

UNCONCERNED, I WENT about trying to upgrade facilities for officers, making the room booking system more transparent and attending to the various issues of the staff and the State Government of J&K.

There were a lot of lady officers working in the PRC. This included an additional secretary, an under-secretary and two fresh KAS recruits functioning as managers. I was really happy that in a *male dominated* J&K, I was working with such lovely female colleagues.

But as soon as I joined—the additional secretary was transferred though she had spent only a short time in the office. I took up the matter with the Chief Secretary but Mr. Asif Khan laughed and told me that I shouldn't waste my breath as nothing would come out of it.

It dawned on me only much later that Mr. Khan was a misogynist who hated women who were officially in equal or superior position to him. The next one to be knocked out was the poor under-secretary. She was under a lot of personal stress as her brother had met with an accident and was undergoing treatment in Delhi for which her help was vital. Her woeful cries were heard by no one in authority and subsequently the State Government of Jammu & Kashmir—*aided and abetted* by Asif Khan— harassed her so much that she resigned from service.

The State of J&K lost a bright young officer but then who cares!

One manager was the relative of a Cabinet Minister from Leh. So, she escaped being thrown out of Delhi. The other manager would hear nasty comments about her looks, weight, etc. from Mr. Khan. She complained to me and I had to pull

Asif Khan up which he didn't take to very kindly. After all, he was distantly related to Mr. Khandey and certainly had his ear.

Mr. Khan's love of life was food and he surrounded himself with corrupt cronies who would indulge him all the time. Also, whenever any important officer landed up in Delhi, he would arrange Biryanis, Kebabs, etc. This was fine except when I was expected to sign bill of 25,000-30,000 rupees for this hospitality. I had to tell Asif Khan that in future he would have to take *prior approval* from me before making such payments or else. This greatly irritated Mr. Asif Khan especially when coming from a lady boss.

Asif's behaviour suddenly became extremely erratic. He wouldn't come to office before 3 p.m. He refused to attend meetings. He was not attending to files which were piling up in his office room. I brought all this in writing to the notice of the Chief Secretary and the Principal Secretary to the Chief Minister, but to no avail.

Once a year, the whole of J&K would descend in Delhi for a meeting in the Planning Commission. Accommodation would invariably run short and then we had to pay through our noses for arranging accommodation in other state *bhavans*. That was becoming difficult to arrange because J&K *Bhavan* didn't believe in reciprocating any such courtesy, that is, when other state level establishments asked for help, J&K House would claim to be "always full" and unable to respond to their needs.

To sort out the issue, I spoke to my batch mate Lalit Pawar who was Chairman of ITDC (India Tourism Development Corporation of the Government of India) and got a wonderful offer for Ashok Hotel. So now I could accommodate officers up to the 1994 batch of IAS, including the Chief Secretary, in Ashok Hotel along with complimentary breakfast at the same rate that we had to pay to other *bhavans*. The officers from the 1995 batch downwards were all accommodated in J&K House itself.

This was all fine on paper except in J&K where even junior officers of 2001 batch belonging to Kashmir considered themselves as *very* senior. In addition, Mr. Asif Khan spread word that I had come up with such a "discriminatory policy" because I was against Kashmiris and Muslims. This was not true because amongst the officers who stayed in the Ashoka Hotel, only three were outsiders, and the rest were from J&K, including Jammu.

The problem was further compounded with the serving of one working lunch. There was a preliminary meeting in the Planning Commission after which all officers had to come to the J&K House at around 12. The Chief Secretary was to hold discussions till 2 p.m. and then all were to proceed again to the Planning Commission for a detailed meeting.

Mr. Khan, as usual, wanted to serve a full wazwan—with at least eight non-veg dishes accompanying his favourite biryani. I did not agree as both financially and logistically it was not possible to organise a wazwan at lunch time in Delhi. Also in my opinion a heavy lunch *shouldn't be* served preceding a very important meeting.

So, while the Chief Secretary was holding the meeting, I got a working lunch consisting of sandwiches from Sugar-and-Spice, baked (and not fried) chips from Pepsi, peanuts and sweets from Haldiram, etc. served. Everyone at that time appreciated the light fare but Mr. Khan was slowly stoking the fire.

So, the inevitable happened. Within 3 months of my joining as PRC, I was *transferred back* to J&K as Chairperson of the Special Tribunal. The local newspaper "Greater Kashmir" reported that I had been transferred for insulting Kashmiri Muslim officers by NOT keeping them in Ashok Hotel and by serving "Moong dal and pea pods" to them for lunch which had infuriated the CM.

What followed next was amazing. This report angered my friends and well-wishers in Kashmir and they spoke to their journalist friends in Delhi. "Mail Today" caught up with me and printed my version of what exactly had happened on the front page. Immediately, all TV channels were full of stories of how I had been transferred for not serving biryani and how sincere and honest officers work at the whims and fancies of their corrupt and incompetent bosses (i.e. politicians and senior bureaucrats) in J&K.

My house was suddenly surrounded by so many Outdoor Broadcasting (OB) vans. Initially, I did not speak to anyone but the young girls who had been asked to cover the story kept waiting in the sweltering heat of Delhi to talk to me. Something within me gave in and I decided to let them enter my house and offered them water. Also, I thought that when my reputation has already been smirched so badly in J&K, let my point of view come across in the national media. And I am really thankful to the media for highlighting the whole issue the way they did.

After this, I was quite sure that the government would take some further nasty action against me. However, nothing happened. Omar and Iqbal had either panicked, or they thought that by dumping me in the Special Tribunal and letting me NOT remain in Delhi, they had already taken their revenge.

Chapter 21

"Punished" to Act as a High Court Judge

THE J&K SPECIAL Tribunal was one of the special institutional creations of Mr. Jagmohan during his brief 6-month Governor's Rule in 1986. Before that, under various Acts, ministers used to be vested with legal powers to revise the orders of functionaries like Financial Commissioner (Revenue) in some land revenue matters, Municipal Commissioners in building permission matters and so on.

Most ministers had neither the training nor the aptitude to deal with such appeals in a legal and judicious manner. So, it was mostly left to their personal staff to type out the judgements depending on which party they wanted to favour and, of course, after extracting an "appropriate compensation."

In one swift stroke, Jagmohan withdrew all such discretionary powers from the ministers and vested them in the Tribunal. The Tribunal had a Chairperson who would move with the annual "Durbar move" but there were two members each who were stationed in Srinagar and Jammu.

One member was from the IAS and the other from the judiciary of the rank of district and sessions judge. The Chairperson had powers of a high court judge and was totally independent of all pressures, at least on paper.

Now, wouldn't holding such a post be wonderful?

Well, not in the dictionary of J&K where political patronage, ability to make transfers and postings, power to get commissions from engineering projects and, of course, the opportunity to go on tours to Delhi mostly for shopping or medical check-ups is considered more important than exercising some judicial functions. Worse was the tag that you have been "punished" for not being a "good girl." So being sent to a boarding school in Baghdad!

It was in that background that I joined the Special Tribunal in August 2013. But as the construction of my house in Greater Noida was still going on, I took some leave to complete it. I seriously began work in the Tribunal from January 2014.

Surprisingly, this assignment turned out to be the best I have ever had. For the first time, I had no boss—I reported neither to the Chief Secretary nor to the Chief Minister nor to any Cabinet Minister. I was a High Court Judge and would hear appeals against the orders of the municipality, the Custodian General for evacuee properties (that is of people who had gone to Pakistan in 1947), the Registrar Cooperative Societies, Commissioner Agrarian Reforms, etc.

Every case was a legal jumble of facts and fiction and slowly I began enjoying my work. This was the first time I was dealing with lawyers as a community—who were not representing me or my department in some other court, but who were representing their clients in MY COURT. In various assignments one had dealt with the Advocate General, Additional Advocate General, etc. but this was so very different.

Because this was supposed to be a *punishment* posting, I found that my predecessors had left a huge backlog of pending cases. The reason, of course, was that in this post, officers were almost always trying desperately to move to the so-called "greener pastures." I, of course, had no such ambitions.

In fact, something strange happened to me. As my mind became calm, my stress levels vanished. Suddenly, I became healthier as all my health parameters became normal. Everyone commented that I looked younger and fitter. What could be a greater blessing than this?

2014 was quite a year. The National elections were held and for the first time in Indian history we had a BJP Government with full majority set to govern the country. Dr. Jitendra Singh from Jammu was elected as Member Parliament (MP) and was made a MOS in the PMO in charge of DOPT.

I was really happy as I had worked closely with him during my tenure in the health and medical education departments. In fact, he had been one of the beneficiaries of my streamlining policy and had got his promotion because of my initiatives. He had actively taken part in the Amarnath agitation on behalf of the Jammu people. He knew us well and had constantly been in touch with us. I was hoping against hope that he would perhaps help us now especially since he was dealing with both DOPT and the PMO. But such hopes never materialise.

Mr. Omar Abdullah, famous for his tweets, had tweeted that in case Mr. Modi became PM, he would leave for Pakistan. *He never did that till this date!*

The Flood Politics

LIFE WENT ON till September when gods really became angry and a devastating flood engulfed Kashmir. Srinagar on the 7th of September 2014 went under water and with it collapsed the already fragile and incompetent civil administration. The Chief Secretary himself was rescued in an inebriated condition and brought to the Hari Niwas Guest House. Officers, ministers and even some members of the judiciary shifted to the Hari Niwas.

Thankfully, we were given those tiny tourist huts at *Cheshma Shahi* and these being on higher grounds did not get submerged. I may mention here that all government accommodation in Srinagar and Jammu has been taken over by politicians and their families and even when they cease to be ministers or even MLAs—no one vacates. So officers, mostly outsiders, who cannot have personal houses in J&K, are given these two room hutments in Srinagar.

A good habit I had developed in J&K was to stock up my kitchen store in a manner that it could see us through for at least a month. Stone throwing and curfew being regular features, we had to have some dry ration, frozen veggies, and tetra pack milk at home as all shops would be closed during such times. This habit really came in handy and helped us survive the flood ordeal.

In fact, it was during this time I realised how much affection some of my sub-ordinates had for us. I was out of vegetables but I found them walking on foot from Ganderbal through a mountainous path to bring me meat and vegetables.

The interesting administrative feature of these floods was that there was both an acute shortage of officers and a desperate need of out-of-box thinking and action. My husband who was Financial Commissioner (Revenue) and head of the revenue machinery that was involved fully in relief work, even went to the extent of driving in his own personal car to Hari Niwas and volunteered to do any work that needed to be assigned to him. However, we were both not involved in any manner.

Later I realised that Mr. Omar Abdullah was ignoring us because he knew we couldn't be party to his mission of adding more and more zeroes to the projections being made to the Government of India for "compensation" for the flood damages! Compensation was in any case a funny word to use as the Government of India gives only "relief" as per set norms during such disasters. But India being the "guilty party" in all matters concerning Kashmir, local papers and politicians kept on shouting for more and more "compensation!"

I could not go to my office as it was submerged under one and a half floors of water. And everything on these floors was totally destroyed. Surprisingly, some orders I had dictated and signed survived inside a Godrej almirah!

When the water subsided, we were left with two feet of muck. The ground floor of the building where my office and court room was located was totally devastated. I, therefore, took a small room on the first floor and began functioning.

My staff and the lawyers were all extremely cooperative, and we were soon able to rebuild many cases which had been destroyed in the floods. In fact, my bonhomie with the Kashmiri advocates really began here. They told me that some anti-nationals had tried to portray me as a *Hindu fundamentalist* especially during the Amarnath agitation. But what they had now realised was—that I was just an excellent officer and a wonderful human being. What a compliment!

Mufti Again

THE DAWN OF 2015 saw the defeat of Mr. Omar Abdullah and the coming together of two opposite parties—the BJP and the PDP. Mr. Mufti Mohammed Sayeed became the CM and, of course, the first people he thanked were militants and Pakistanis while the Deputy CM Mr. Nirmal Singh from the BJP sat next to him and remained mum. This was a harbinger of what was to follow.

Mr. Mufti did meet me and praised me for having done yeoman service in the education, health and industries sector. He also declared that I couldn't be left in the Special Tribunal because he had more important work for me. Of course, this was never to be and I at the fag end of my career was beyond caring.

Generally, with any regime change, there is a reshuffle of the bureaucracy. But not this time. Mr. Omar Abdullah's favourites proved to be the favourites of Mr. Mufti and he retained all of them in the same position, including the Chief Secretary and the Principal Secretary to the CM. Wow, what a continuity!

The inertia and mal-administration which was a symbol of Mr. Abdullah's governance, therefore, continued. From the side lines, I was watching with amusement.

Things, however, suddenly started heating up. Mr. Iqbal Khandey, who so far had been identified as part of PDP, suddenly put in his papers three months before retirement. He stated that he couldn't continue if instead of Chief Secretary the government wanted him to act as a mere "chief stenographer."

The "Outsiders" Lose Again

FOR A WEEK, there was no Chief Secretary in J&K. Then the rumours started.

The local newspapers started saying that the next senior most officer in the IAS was Mr. B.R. Sharma (1984 IAS JK) and that he would soon be taking over. This was, of course, an orchestrated campaign to ignore Arun who was next in seniority to Iqbal, and **FIVE YEARS** senior to B. R. Sharma. Arun also had one and a half years to go before retirement.

There were three other seniors who were being superseded. Excluding me, there was Ashok Angurana (1980 IAS JK) who was working in the Government of India, and Khurshid Ganai (1982 IAS JK) who was serving the State Government. True, Khurshid was to retire end of October 2015 and I would be retiring by the end of November but Arun still had a long way to go. Can a person five years junior *supersede* us all?

Mr. B.R. Sharma was, of course, a well-entrenched local officer with relatives all over the business, bureaucratic and political spectrum. He was initially allotted West Bengal cadre, and only much later after using a great deal of political influence was his cadre changed to J&K. Once again in "public interest!"

Anyway, speculations ran high, but we knew it was a losing battle. Mufti did exactly what he was famous for—a total disregard of the IAS cadre rules and seniority. The *stupid* BJP members whose rise to fame was largely attributed to Mr.

Modi, and to Arun, who had supposedly opened their eyes on the Amarnath issue, behaved like a local parochial party. They were now just a B-team of the PDP and there was nothing nationalist about them.

"Yes, yes, make our Jammu local boy CS—Country and All-India Service be damned!"

And so, the "curse of the outsider" fell on us again with a force that left us reeling. For the first time in the history of IAS in India, a five-year junior who was still NOT in the Chief Secretary's pay grade, superseded four seniors and became the Chief Secretary.

We thought we should immediately put in our papers, take two-days to pack up our Srinagar stuff, move to Jammu, take another week to pack up the Jammu stuff, and shift to our near-complete house in Greater Noida. General Sinha, our ex-Governor, rang up to express his sympathies and said he knew that after the Amarnath imbroglio Mufti would have never made Arun the CS. As for us resigning, he thought that would be an honourable thing to do as he too had resigned when the Indira Gandhi Government had bypassed him for the post of the Army Chief.

Madhav Lal (1977 IAS JK) too rang up and drilled some sense in to us. Our retirement papers were still far from complete, the 7th Pay Commission Report was expected any day, and Arun could be given a "face-saving" posting in which he may not have to report to his 5-year junior Chief Secretary. Resigning in a huff could have created complications on all these fronts. Many other seniors rang up with similar advice.

Arun was soon made Vice Chairman and Director General of IMPA (Institute of Management and Public Administration), an inconsequential post, but with the powers of the Chief Secretary. And so we lumped up the *insult* and ploughed on pursuing our retirement papers. Papers which in the Government of India are completed by the office in routine, in an elaborate process that kicks in some eighteen months before any officer retires.

First, we had to get our "service verified" from every office we had served so far. Then, get our leave record reconciled. Next, get details of every deduction of our car loan, housing loan, General Provident Fund, and General Insurance reconciled. Fourth, get a certificate from the secretariat library that no books are shown outstanding against our name. Fifth, from the Estates that we have returned all furniture issued to us, and so on.

There were some 20-odd things that we had to pursue! The harassment is so severe that many outsider officers just give up and go away WITHOUT getting their provident fund and insurance dues. But I didn't allow J&K to get away from their responsibilities that easily and had my Pension, Gratuity, Insurance and Leave Encashment orders in my hand two months before I retired. That I believe was quite a record!

I finally retired from the IAS on the 30th of November 2015 and was deeply touched by the farewells I got. Lawyers came from Srinagar to give me a party in Jammu. Jammu lawyers showered me with some token gifts and, of course, my Special Tribunal members and staff had parties after parties. Frankly, I was totally bowled over by this gesture as this is something very uncommon in J&K and certainly NOT in the Tribunal.

The IAS Officers Association also wanted to give me a farewell party as I had been their ex-Secretary and President but here internal politics took over. Those who wanted to be in the good books of the new 5-year junior Chief Secretary split the ranks. Still some 20 IAS officers got together in their private capacity to give me a farewell in a private hotel in Jammu. Most of these officers were from very junior batches and I must express my gratitude to them.

Maybe they thought they could still find something to learn from my long and arduous journey in the IAS.

Epilogue

AS I LOOK out of the bay windows of my house in Greater Noida, I marvel at the blue sky and the two beautiful *Kareel (Capparis Decidua)* trees right in front laden with striking-red flowers. And what are those smaller-than-sparrow birds drinking nectar with their long beaks? Oh God, they are Humming Birds! I had never seen them in my life, not in Kashmir, Jammu or Ladakh, and here I find them frolicking in my own backyard in the Delhi-NCR region!

I was so scared of the pollution here that I had purchased a Laser Egg air quality monitor, two room air purifiers, a car air purifier, and dozens of industrial-grade PM 2.5 masks *while* in J&K. But now when I compare the dust and pollution level in and around my house with what I had in Jammu and Kashmir, I find the air actually cleaner here! The night skies too are clearer where I can see stars easily.

Scared of the unscheduled power cuts, I have invested in invertors, batteries, and roof-top solar PV panels. But the blackouts don't last for more than 15 minutes on an average every day.

I thought no one will recognise me here. But my Society, two months before I was to come, elected me unopposed as their Secretary. People greet me when we go for our morning and evening walks as they used to in J&K.

I didn't know who will get my gas cylinders re-filled here, but I actually have piped gas supply in my kitchen. Without any office support, I thought I'll have hell of a problem paying my telephone, electricity, gas, and TV bills, but thanks to the digital revolution I can pay all of these on-line. Why, I don't have to pay in cash even for my veggies or groceries here in the nearby air-conditioned supermarkets, which was unthinkable in J&K.

I do, of course, miss my 5-km morning walk, during the summer months, to the *Parimahal* from our little hut in *Cheshma Shahi* in Srinagar, which according to my Fitbit amounted to climbing 32 floors, EVERY DAY. I also miss the uphill climb from the *Bagh-i-Bahu* garden to the *Bahu* Fort, and the breath-taking view of Jammu city from the top every winter morning from November to March. The walk in the park next door in Greater Noida is such a poor substitute.

I miss the call of the Cuckoo bird in Srinagar in April-May, but the *Koel* bird here compensates for that a little. Above all, I miss my friends, colleagues, and acquaintances who have been so kind to us when we were in J&K.

But otherwise, there is such a sense of all-pervading relief after retirement. There would be no more packing for "Durbar Moves" every six months. No fear of opening my cartons and finding my TV or music system or microwave or crockery chipped or broken. No sub-optimal life in Srinagar where you can't use a washing machine to wash your clothes, or a home-theatre to watch your movies, or air conditioners to tame the stifling weather of July-August, or even a chimney to draw out the fumes from your kitchen.

There would be no overstocking of milk, spices and dry rations, lest strikes, stone pelting and curfews stop my movement to the bazaars in Kashmir. No tension whether I'd be able to reach the airport the day I have to take a flight out.

No strange stares at your bindi and saree as if you have come from some other planet. No blood-curdling chants of

"Hum Kya Chahe Azaadi" and *"Allahu-Akbar"* in Kashmir and the ear-splitting cacophony of DJs and all-night non-stop *Jagratas* in Jammu.

And above all, no rubbing in my "outsiderness" and "non-State subjectness" again and again. No more being superseded by locals five-years our junior. No more hoping that rules will change some day and I will be able to own a 1-room hut along the Aru river in Kashmir or in Patnitop in Jammu. No more hoping that my son will be able to study in a medical or engineering college in J&K or hope to be employed by the State Government there, or even get married to a local girl.

I have borne this curse of being an outsider with stoicism and equanimity and lived to tell the tale.

But can J&K survive the curse of us outsiders so equally well?

This is what I need to see now.

Index